S0-BMS-314

DISCARDED

BEDFORD
FREE PUBLIC
LIBRARY
BEDFORD, MASSACHUSETTS

The
**BEDFORD
FLAG**
*The oldest
flag in the
United States*

The Bedford Flag, commissioned to Cornet John Page
in 1737 by King George II of England, was carried by his
son, Nathaniel, who fought with the Bedford Minutemen
at the Battle of Concord Bridge, April 19, 1775.

Acquired _____ DEC 1969 _____ No. 64158

THE KINGDOM OF GOD
AND PRIMITIVE CHRISTIANITY

ALBERT SCHWEITZER

—————

The Kingdom of God
and
Primitive Christianity

EDITED, WITH AN INTRODUCTION, BY
ULRICH NEUENSCHWANDER

TRANSLATED BY L. A. GARRARD

THE SEABURY PRESS
New York

FIRST SEABURY EDITION PUBLISHED 1968

COPYRIGHT © 1967 RHENA ECKERT-SCHWEITZER
TRANSLATION COPYRIGHT © 1968 A. AND C. BLACK, LTD., LONDON

LIBRARY OF CONGRESS CATALOG CARD NUMBER: 68-24007
606-868-C-5
PRINTED IN THE UNITED STATES OF AMERICA

All rights reserved. No part of this book may be used or reproduced in any manner whatsoever without written permission from the publisher except in the case of brief quotations embodied in critical articles and reviews.

INTRODUCTION

After the death of Albert Schweitzer his daughter discovered in Lambaréné, packed in a white linen bag, the manuscript of this last theological work of his, *The Kingdom of God and Primitive Christianity*. It is not so much an exposition of the meaning of the idea of the Kingdom of God for present-day Christianity as an historical investigation of the biblical belief in the Kingdom from the Old Testament prophets to the Apostle Paul. The heart of the book lies in the chapters on Jesus and Paul, concerned with the field which has always been the centre of Schweitzer's research. Here he gives once more an exposition from the point of view of the Kingdom of his thorough-going eschatological interpretation of the Gospels. In contrast, however, with his former monographs on *The Quest of the Historical Jesus* and *The Mysticism of the Apostle Paul*, in this survey his scope extends back over late Judaism to the beginnings of belief in the Kingdom and the preaching of the prophet Amos concerning the Day of Yahweh.

The substance of the book was written in the years 1950–51. Almost every page is dated, and we are thus enabled to trace the growth of the MS. with considerable precision. The great opportunity to work it out came with the voyage to Europe in May and June 1951. Schweitzer found on board ship the time and leisure so seldom available to him for the final composition of the text. Although the MS. now published was lying practically ready for the printer, Schweitzer never published it. It was his intention to extend the inquiry further still. It is probably impossible to determine how far beyond Paul he intended to extend his survey; it may have been down to the establishment of the early Catholic Church, or even in a grand sweep of thought right down to the present day. No outline of the whole work has yet come to light.

All that is certain is that some extension was planned. We possess sketches of the plan of a further chapter dealing with the recession of eschatology, using the later New Testament writings as material. Albert Schweitzer began to write this chapter on

15th June, 1951, after his arrival at Günsbach, but never made any further progress with the work.

What we have before us is therefore the first and completed part of a work designed to encompass a wider range. It is a portion complete in itself, not merely an outline. This is quite clear from the fact that Schweitzer has frequently made corrections and marked the corrected chapters with the word "Definitive", whereas those which exist only in outline are marked "Provisional". Schweitzer worked through this final version of the completed portion on the ship before he passed on to the first sketches of the second part. The end of the chapter on Paul therefore marks a certain concluding point and shows us how basic was the importance that Schweitzer attached to the Apostle's thought on the Kingdom. It is more than a transitional conclusion: here we have the authentic expression of fundamental insights of abiding importance. Where for Schweitzer Paul marked a caesura, we now have the final conclusion of the book.

The Kingdom of God and Primitive Christianity may be called in a sense Albert Schweitzer's theological testament. Compared with his other works, it is important in two respects:

1. Schweitzer here brings together in a popular presentation his survey of the biblical belief in the Kingdom of God. Previously he had developed his thorough-going eschatological view either in books of technical theology, whose extensive apparatus of learning made them somewhat inaccessible to the non-specialist public, or else in quite general references, such as those found in his autobiography, *From My Life and Thought*.

The book which lies before us, on the other hand, is designed to introduce the basic ideas of Albert Schweitzer's understanding of Jesus to a wider, non-theological public. This is all the more desirable because outside the circle of specialist theologians only the vaguest conception of his views prevails. Furthermore this inquiry, while it makes no pretence of conveying any essentially new ideas, provides the specialists with the comprehensive survey which has hitherto been missing.

2. *The Kingdom of God and Primitive Christianity* provides us with an insight into the theological development of Schweitzer

extending into his extreme old age. It is clear from the MS. how intensely he remains a biblical theologian even to the end of his days. It shows that to the end he stood firmly by his basic views, looking upon his work not as a crisis of theology, but as a helpful development of it. There is an amazing consistency in the way in which his theological thought in the work of his old age centres round the same major questions as that of his youthful studies: the Kingdom of God and the preaching of Jesus and the Apostle Paul.

It is the last work of an old man dwelling in the loneliness of the primeval forest. The book gives the feeling of having been written not in the hurly-burly of academic life but in the quietness of seclusion. Here is a man who has nothing in front of him but the text of the Bible, on which he is reflecting. It is a striking fact that in the whole exposition there is no note of controversy, not even a reference to all the discussion that has been going on among New Testament scholars since the 'thirties. There is no confrontation with the questions raised by Form Criticism. The few references Schweitzer makes to other theologians relate to scholars who were writing at the time when Schweitzer himself held an academic post. It would have been extremely interesting to learn something about Schweitzer's attitude towards the latest conclusions of Form Criticism, especially since the scholars of this school have abandoned their earlier radical rejection and are now once again approaching his problem of "the historical Jesus". It was, however, naturally impossible for Schweitzer to deal with the whole literature concerning Form Criticism. Even if he had been technically equipped to undertake it, it is hardly likely that he would have made the attempt. The whole conception of the book is purely expository and in no way polemical: it is concerned solely with the theme itself. In its whole design it is a work written in the loneliness of the primeval forest. That is how it should be and is meant to be read; not merely as a work of scholarship, but also as one which calls the reader to reflection and leads him into the presence of Jesus Christ.

Zollikofen, near Bern   ULRICH NEUENSCHWANDER

TRANSLATOR'S PREFACE

It is a privilege to be able to assist in bringing Albert Schweitzer's "theological testament" in *Reich Gottes und Christentum* before the English-speaking public. It is over half a century since *The Quest of the Historical Jesus* burst upon the theological world, and many who have never read that impressive work, and have perhaps been daunted by the detailed survey of German literature on the life of Jesus which occupied so large a part of it, may be glad to read this considered statement of Schweitzer's own views, written in the serenity of his old age.

A few changes in presentation have been made from the German edition. A large part of the book appears there in small type; here a uniform size of type has been used for the text, one or two of the small-type passages being placed in footnotes. Two or three of the notes have been omitted altogether, usually because they dealt with linguistic points connected with German versions of the Bible, which would have been both unfamiliar and meaningless to English readers. Some liberties have also been taken with the paragraph arrangement, to avoid the strange appearance of a number of very short paragraphs on the same page. A few additions have been made to the useful index of passages prepared for the German edition by Mr. Schmocker, Assistant to the Theological Faculty at the University of Bern, and a further index of proper names has been added by the translator.

After careful consideration it was decided that biblical quotations should be taken from the Revised Version of 1881; this is probably the most familiar to readers in Britain, though not in America. In a number of important passages it is closer to Schweitzer's German rendering, and so more relevant to his argument, than the Revised Standard Version. Quotations from the Old Testament Pseudepigrapha are usually taken from R.H. Charles's *The Apocrypha and Pseudepigrapha of the Old Testament*.

In conclusion, I wish to express my gratitude to the Principal and Council of Manchester College, Oxford, for the hospitality and facilities placed at my disposal during the summer vacation, without which the translation could not have been completed within the allotted time.

Emerson College
Boston
Massachusetts

L. A. GARRARD

CONTENTS

I. THE KINGDOM OF GOD IN THE PROPHETS AND IN LATE JUDAISM

THE KINGDOM OF GOD
AND PRIMITIVE CHRISTIANITY

CHAPTER I

THE KINGDOM OF GOD IN THE PROPHETS AND IN LATE JUDAISM

1. THE KINGDOM OF GOD IN THE PRE-EXILIC PROPHETS

Amos

Christianity is essentially a religion of belief in the coming of the Kingdom of God. It begins with the message preached by John the Baptist on the banks of the Jordan, "Repent, for the Kingdom of Heaven is at hand" (Mt. 3 : 2). It was with the same preaching that Jesus came forward in Galilee after the imprisonment of the Baptist (Mt. 4 : 12, 17).

The Christian view of the Kingdom of God arises out of the Jewish. For this reason a knowledge of the expectation of the Kingdom of God found in the Prophets and in late Judaism is essential if we are to understand the background of the thought of John the Baptist, Jesus, Paul and the earliest Christians.

The idea of the Kingdom of God is the creation of the Jewish prophets. It developed out of the notion of the Day of Yahweh. The original idea of this was that God was to execute judgement on the nations against whom his chosen people Israel had been compelled to maintain themselves in a series of fierce struggles ever since their settlement in Palestine, and that he would subject these peoples to Israel for all time. A reign of peace was expected, in which the mastery of the world would fall to the people of Israel.

This picture of the Day of Yahweh is challenged by the prophet Amos. At the time of his appearance the unified Kingdom of Israel had ceased to exist. After the death of Solomon (about 933 B.C.) it had fallen apart into two separate kingdoms, one in the south, the Kingdom of Judah, ruled by the descendants of David, and one in the north, consisting of ten tribes and ruled by kings drawn from these. Amos was a herdsman and dresser of fig-mulberries at Tekoa in Judah. Here he experienced the call to be a prophet about 760, at the time when Jeroboam II (783–743) was ruler of the Northern Kingdom. He appeared at Bethel, the holy city of this kingdom.

According to his preaching, the Day of Yahweh would be quite different from what men imagined. God's judgement would be executed not only upon the enemies of his people but upon the people itself as well. Because Yahweh is an ethical God, to show himself as such he must execute judgement upon all peoples, including the people which belongs to him in a special way, and the verdict will be based solely on the good or evil of their deeds. In the speech which comes first in the biblical record of his preaching Amos recounts the deeds of shame committed by the Aramaeans, the Philistines, the Phoenicians, the Edomites, the Ammonites and the Moabites through their atrocities in war (Amos 1 : 1–2 : 3). For these God will destroy their cities and cause their lands to become a wilderness.

The speech continues with a promise of punishment to Judah and Israel too. God reproaches them for thinking that because of the sacrifices which they offer him he must be favourably disposed towards them. He cannot be, for they do not do the things that are really pleasing to him. They pervert justice and deal unmercifully with the poor. Therefore God will deliver them into the hands of their enemies, who will lead them into captivity. It is not his will that they should be completely annihilated. If they turn to him, he will have mercy upon them. A remnant of his people is to be saved and will live and rule in the glorious Kingdom of peace which will break upon them. The Day of Yahweh will be not a day of victory but a day of sifting. "You only have I known of all the families of the earth: therefore I will visit upon you all your iniquities" (Amos 3 : 2). "Woe unto you that desire the day of the Lord! Wherefore would ye have the day of the Lord? . . . Shall not the day of the Lord be darkness, and not light? Even very dark, and no brightness in it? I hate, I despise your feasts, and I will take no delight in your solemn assemblies. Yea, though ye offer me your burnt offerings and meal offerings, I will not accept them: neither will I regard the peace offerings of your fat beasts. Take thou away from me the noise of thy songs;

for I will not hear the melody of thy viols. But let judgement roll down as waters, and righteousness as a mighty stream" (Amos 5 : 18, 20–24). "Seek good, and not evil, that ye may live: and so the Lord, the God of hosts, shall be with you, as ye say. Hate the evil, and love the good, and establish judgement in the gate: it may be that the Lord, the God of hosts, will be gracious unto the remnant of Joseph" (Amos 5 : 14 f.). "Israel shall surely be led away captive out of his land" (Amos 7 : 17). "I will not utterly destroy the house of Jacob, saith the Lord. For, lo, I will command, and I will sift the house of Israel among all the nations, like as corn is sifted in a sieve. . . . All the sinners of my people shall die by the sword, which say, The evil shall not overtake nor prevent us" (Amos 9 : 8–10). "In that day will I raise up the tabernacle of David that is fallen, and close up the breaches thereof; and I will raise up his ruins, and I will build it as in the days of old. . . . And I will plant them upon their land, and they shall no more be plucked up out of their land which I have given them, saith the Lord thy God" (Amos 9 : 11, 15).

In these tremendous utterances the knowledge of the completely ethical personality of God is for the first time made known, and it follows that ethical thought and action alone give the right to a place in the coming Kingdom of God.

Amos begins the succession of prophets who record their preaching in writing. His great religious achievement is based upon that of two predecessors who lived a century earlier in the Northern Kingdom, Elijah under King Ahab (876–854) and Elisha in the time of King Joram (853–842). They had testified against the practice of worshipping the Baals as the deities of the land of Canaan alongside of Yahweh, the God of the people of Israel, and offering sacrifice to them as the givers of the fruit of the soil. They had striven to set men free from the feeling of dependence on these gods and to lead them to worship Yahweh alone. They did not emphasize his ethical character as yet. They based his uniqueness solely on the fact that he was the God of Israel and the only God with real might. In this way they laid the foundations of monotheism. In raising Yahweh above all gods of all nations they were establishing the conditions for insight into his even higher uniqueness as completely ethical personality.

Elijah and Elisha were zealous for the purity of worship of Yahweh. For Amos the cultus no longer has any meaning. It does not create any relationship between man and God: only moral action does this. The cultic reverence for Yahweh demanded by his two forerunners turns in Amos into an ethical reverence. The change means a spiritualization of religion which has never since been lost.

The ideas of Amos underlie the preaching of the prophets who followed him. In the Northern Kingdom Hosea appeared between 750 and 740. In the Southern we hear the voice of Isaiah (740–710), Micah (in the time of King Hezekiah, 727–699), Zephaniah (under King Josiah, 640–609) and Jeremiah (628–586). Like Amos, these prophets expect that God will punish his people for their misdeeds by sending them into exile and destroying all but a small remnant, out of which the people will arise again.

The Northern Kingdom experienced this fate in 722 B.C. The capture of Samaria by the Assyrian King Sargon (722–706) meant the end. A large part of the population was transplanted to Assyria and Media. The Kingdom of Judah enjoyed over a century's respite.

Isaiah: The Messiah of David's Line

Isaiah, the most important of the prophets who followed Amos, admonishes the people to see the power of God in all the events of history and submit to it, not attempting to resist, either in their own strength or in alliance with other powers. Isaiah, too, is convinced that in the end a remnant of the people of Judah will be saved. The Kingdom of Peace cannot break through until the people have been punished by God for their sins. The full development of this idea of the Kingdom of Peace in Isaiah is that it will have for its ruler a king of the house of David, armed with the Spirit of God. "For unto us a child is born, unto us a son is given; and the government shall be upon his shoulder.... Of the increase of his government and of peace there shall be no end, upon the throne of David, and upon his kingdom . . . from henceforth even for ever" (Is. 9 : 6 f.). "And there shall come forth a shoot out of the stock of Jesse, and a branch out of his roots shall bear fruit: and the spirit of the Lord shall rest upon him, the spirit of wisdom and understanding, the spirit of counsel and might, the spirit of knowledge and of the fear of the Lord; and his delight shall be in the fear of the Lord: and he shall not judge after the sight of his eyes, neither reprove after the hearing of his ears: but with righteousness shall he judge the poor, and reprove with equity for the meek of the earth: and he shall smite the earth with the rod of his mouth, and with the breath of his lips shall he slay the wicked" (Is. 11 : 1–4).

This ruler of the Kingdom, coming of the line of David, is described by the term the Messiah (the Anointed). He is anointed as its king by God himself through the gift of his Spirit. By divine commission Samuel had anointed Saul as king by pouring oil upon his head (1 Sam. 10 : 1) and he did the same later with David (1 Sam. 16 : 12 f.).

Another new element in Isaiah's teaching is that at the time of the appearance of the Kingdom of God there will be a transformation in nature, as a result of which the creatures will give up their former manner of life, so that they and men alike shall conform to the way of peace. "And the wolf shall dwell with the lamb and the leopard shall lie down with the kid; and the calf and the young lion and the fatling together; and a little child shall lead them. And the cow and the bear shall feed; their young ones shall lie down together: and the lion shall eat straw like the ox. . . . They shall not hurt nor destroy in all my holy mountain: for the earth shall be full of the knowledge of the Lord, as the waters cover the sea" (Is. 11 : 6–9). The expectation that at the time of the Kingdom of Peace God will also transform the natural world appears with ever-increasing emphasis in the later prophets.

Jeremiah: The Messianic Kingdom brought about by the Spirit of God

Jeremiah was active in the terrible time which preceded the destruction of Jerusalem. Like Isaiah, he tells the people that they must not rebel against what God sends them. Before 609 Judah was a vassal state of Egypt. After the Battle of Carchemish (605), in which the Egyptians were defeated by Nebuchadnezzar, King of Babylon (605–562), it was in subjection to the Babylonians (Chaldaeans). Jeremiah preaches that it is God's will that they shall submit to this rule. An attempt at rebellion against it resulted in the immediate surrender of Jerusalem by King Jehoiachin, who had come to the throne in 597. Thousands of members of the leading Jewish families were carried off to Babylon. Jehoiachin's brother Zedekiah was installed as king in 597, after promising loyalty to Nebuchadnezzar. Disregarding Jeremiah's warnings, he rose in 588, relying on the help of Egypt. During the eighteen months' siege Jeremiah never ceased to preach that it was God's will that Nebuchadnezzar should take the city, and that all resistance ought to be abandoned as hopeless. "Thus saith the Lord: Behold I set before you the way of life and the way of death. He that abideth in this city shall die by the sword, and by the famine, and by the pestilence: but he that goeth out, and falleth away to the Chaldeans that besiege you, he shall live, and his life shall be unto him for a prey. For I have set my face upon this city for evil, and not for good, saith the Lord: it shall be given into the hand of the king of Babylon, and he shall burn it with fire" (Jer. 21 : 8–10). Because of this prophecy Jeremiah was imprisoned.

After the capture of the city in 586 the sons of Zedekiah were killed before his eyes, along with the leading men in Judah. Zedekiah was blinded and brought to Babylon in chains. Jerusalem was burned to the ground. The majority of the inhabitants had to move to Babylon, only a few of the poorest people, who had nothing they could call their own (Jer. 39 : 10), being allowed to stay behind. Jeremiah was permitted by the commander of Nebuchadnezzar's troops to choose whether he would come to Babylon or stay in the land. A crowd of refugees fleeing to Egypt compelled him to go with them and he probably died in Egypt shortly afterwards.

The reason why Jeremiah could expect the people to accept patiently as something sent by God all the misfortunes they had to endure was that these events were trivial compared with the time which would follow the testing. It was of no real consequence whether Judah was for a few years an independent kingdom or a vassal of the Chaldaeans. The only thing that mattered was what would become of it when the humiliation gave place to the exaltation. This is the future which he never ceases to hold before the people's eyes.

The new age will begin with the return of all God's people who have been in captivity, whether they belonged to the Kingdom of Israel or to that of Judah. "I will cause the captivity of Judah and the captivity of Israel to return. . . . And I will cleanse them from all their iniquity, whereby they have sinned against me; and I will pardon all their iniquities" (Jer. 33 : 7 f.).

Like Isaiah, Jeremiah expects that a king of the house of David will hold sway in the Kingdom of Peace. With him, however, side by side with the idea of the coming Kingdom appears that of the new covenant. It is not only the king but the people too who will be vehicles of the Holy Spirit. For him the Kingdom consists in a new and higher covenant which God will make with his people. "Behold, the days come, saith the Lord, that I will raise unto David a righteous Branch, and he shall reign as king and deal wisely, and shall execute judgement and justice in the land. In his days Judah shall be saved, and Israel shall dwell safely" (Jer. 23 : 5 f.). "Behold, the days come, saith the Lord, that I will make a new covenant with the house of Israel, and with the house of Judah: not according to the covenant that I made with their fathers in the day that I took them by the hand to bring them out of the land of Egypt; which my covenant they brake, although I was an husband unto them, saith the Lord. But this is the covenant that I will make with the house of Israel after those days, saith the Lord; I will put my law in their inward parts, and in their heart will I write it; and I will be their God, and they shall be my people: and they shall teach no more every man his neighbour, and every man his brother, saying, Know the Lord: for they shall all know me, from the least of them unto the greatest of them" (Jer. 31 : 31–34).

Because of this addition to the concept of the new Davidic

Kingdom of that of the new covenant, there arises in Jeremiah an ethical conception of the coming Kingdom that is not to be found, at any rate in the same depth and inwardness, in the earlier prophets. He is the first to rise to the recognition that the essence of the Kingdom of God lies in the fact that men's success comes from God, that their thought and action are the operation of his Spirit.

Jeremiah's view of the fate of the other nations and their relation to God's people in the coming age is that God has mercy upon them too and will give them an opportunity to serve him as the true God. "Thus saith the Lord against all mine evil neighbours, that touch the inheritance which I have caused my people Israel to inherit: Behold, I will pluck them up from off their land, and will pluck up the house of Judah from among them. And it shall come to pass, after that I have plucked them up, I will return and have compassion on them; and I will bring them again, every man to his heritage, and every man to his land. And it shall come to pass, if they will diligently learn the ways of my people, to swear by my name, As the Lord liveth; even as they taught my people to swear by Baal; then shall they be built up in the midst of my people. But if they will not hear, then will I pluck up that nation, plucking up and destroying it, saith the Lord" (Jer. 12 : 14–17). Jeremiah expects, therefore, that the Gentiles too may succeed in sharing in the coming Kingdom. This idea persists in the expectation of the generations that follow.

That Judaism should rise from the expectation that God will place their enemies in subjection to them to the higher view that in the end he will treat them in the same way as the Jews themselves means a change for which the way had already been paved in Amos. He had risen to the view, not present in the original concept of the Day of Yahweh, that God will judge his people in that day as he does their gentile oppressors, on the basis of whether they have chosen good or evil. Equality in condemnation necessarily carries with it equality in grace. The development of the expectation of God's people from particularism to universalism is based upon the ethical conception of God.

Ezekiel

Ezekiel is the first representative of a type of prophecy which includes elaborately conceived visions and symbolic actions. It no longer possesses the moving simplicity of an Amos or Isaiah.

A member of the Jerusalem priesthood, he came to Babylon with the first group of exiles in 597. From 593 to 573 he was active as a prophet among his fellow-captives. Ezekiel is sensitive to the problem implicit in the idea of the salvation of a remnant of the people, from whom a people well-pleasing to God will be reconstituted. If this is how the remnant is defined, it is difficult to see how it can consist of both good and evil individuals who happen to have survived. It would be more natural to suppose that it is constituted of the good alone and so has a built-in tendency to become the new people well-pleasing to God.

Ezekiel does in fact put this view forward in a vision referring to the imminent capture of Jerusalem. He sees God giving to a heavenly being in the streets of the city the commission to traverse them, making a mark on the foreheads of "the men who sigh and groan over all the abominations that are committed" in the city. This figure commissioned by God is followed by others, who are commanded to slay and to leave alive only those who bear this mark on their forehead (Ezk. 9 : 1–7).

Ezekiel's contemporary Jeremiah takes a different view of the way in which salvation comes about. With an eye to the imminent capture of Jerusalem he preaches to the besieged that those who go out and give themselves up to the Chaldaeans will remain alive (Jer. 21 : 8 f.). Two completely different views of the deliverance thus underlie the teaching of the two contemporary prophets, both of whose preaching deals with the same event. Jeremiah's point of view is simple, concerned with the actual facts of the situation. In Ezekiel the deliverance is a matter of election and preservation by God, out of which will emerge a remnant of the people well-pleasing to him.

The older prophets had been concerned only with the corporate personality of the people, whereas Ezekiel is concerned with the individual as well. He cannot simply leave the latter to share in the punishment and resurrection of the people, but feels the need to understand the way in which they share in it as part of God's will. It is through him that the notion of care for the individual finds its place in eschatological expectation. Those who have escaped with their life and come from Jerusalem to Babylon as captives are for him a body of the elect. The captives who are already in Babylon as a result of the first displacement will have to take account of this. "They shall come forth unto you, and ye shall see their way and their doings: and ye shall be comforted concerning the evil that I have brought upon Jerusalem" (Ezk. 14 : 22). In Ezekiel as in Jeremiah the idea of the new covenant and that of the king of David's line to whom God will entrust the rule are found together side by side.

Ezekiel: The Final Tribulation. The New Jerusalem

On the question of the cultus as a way of honouring God, he adopts a different position from that of his predecessors. Following the lead of Amos, they teach that the only true worship of God is to walk according to his will. They will allow no significance to the cultus. Ezekiel, the prophet who comes of a priestly family, seeks to replace the false cultus with the true. His attitude is that when God has brought his people back to Canaan he will graciously accept the sacrifices offered to him in Zion.

What is peculiar to Ezekiel is the notion that in the era of the new Kingdom an enemy will once more arise against Israel, an enemy from the extreme North, Gog from the land of Magog. God himself will direct him against the land of Israel, in order to destroy him there and so reveal himself as the Holy One before the eyes of the people. He will then prepare a sacrificial meal of the flesh and blood of the mighty for the birds and all the beasts of the field on the mountains of Israel (Ezk. 38 : 1–39 : 29). This idea probably arose under the influence of the great danger that the invasions of the Scythians were presenting to the contemporary Orient.

In a group of prophecies from the year 573, thirteen years after the destruction of Jerusalem, Ezekiel describes on the basis of visions the new Jerusalem and the new temple. At the same time, in accordance with revelations he has received, he gives instructions on the rite of sacrifice as it will be offered in the future (Ezk. 40–48). It is a striking fact that he, who had lived in Jerusalem and known the Temple when it was still standing, takes no account of the given configuration of the ground in his design for the new Jerusalem and the new temple, but depicts the city as a great square with twelve gates, three on each side, and the temple area as a square lying within it. He must be assuming that the ground will acquire the shape needed for the new Jerusalem. Another change will be that under the temple building a spring gushes forth, whose water miraculously forms a river flowing into the Dead Sea and making its salt water healthy, so that it will be plentiful in fish. On the banks of the river fruit-trees with leaves that never wither will grow and bear fresh fruit every month (Ezk. 47 : 1–12).

The expectation of the Day of Yahweh as we know it from Amos presupposes only an intervention of God in the course of history. In Isaiah there occurs also a transformation in living nature, in so far as the creatures are granted a way of life which gives them the possibility of sharing in the Kingdom of Peace (Is. 11 : 6–9). In Ezekiel inanimate nature also achieves a transformation from a state of imperfection to one of perfection. The hope of the miraculous becomes increasingly prominent in the expectation of the future.

Deutero-Isaiah (Is. 40–66): The Future Glory

In the year 538, twenty-five years after the last prophecies of Ezekiel, the Persian King Cyrus (538–529), after conquering Babylon, published an edict allowing the Jews to return to their country.

Speeches of an unknown prophet referring to this event are

preserved for us in the second part of the Book of Isaiah (Is. 40–66). In the biblical tradition they have been added to the Book of Isaiah, though they make no claim to be the work of the prophet Isaiah and carry clear traces of the time when they arose. They take it for granted that Jerusalem lies in ruins, that the people are in captivity in Babylonia, and they name Koresh (Cyrus) as their liberator. To give their author a name, these twenty-seven chapters that have been added to the Book of Isaiah are called the work of Deutero-Isaiah (the second Isaiah). The preaching ot Deutero-Isaiah takes the form of hymns on the imminenf redemption of Israel. He is a poet-prophet.

These hymns look forward to the return of the people seen as a completely supernatural event. God will lead those who return to Jerusalem. Nature will give expression to its joy at their good fortune and make itself serviceable to them by his command. The new Jerusalem will be like a home in another world. "Comfort ye, comfort ye my people, saith your God. Speak ye comfortably to Jerusalem, and cry unto her, that her warfare is accomplished, that her iniquity is pardoned; that she hath received of the Lord's hand double for all her sins. The voice of one that crieth, Prepare ye in the wilderness the way of the Lord, make straight in the desert a high way for our God. Every valley shall be exalted, and every mountain and hill shall be made low: and the crooked shall be made straight, and the rough places plain: and the glory of the Lord shall be revealed" (Is. 40 : 1–5). Those who have been scattered abroad will return home from the four corners of the world. The Gentiles will conduct them home, build the walls of Jerusalem and offer gifts to the city of God. "Surely the isles shall wait for me, and the ships of Tarshish first, to bring thy sons from far, their silver and their gold with them. . . . And strangers shall build up thy walls, and their kings shall minister unto thee. . . . Thy gates also shall be open continually; they shall not be shut day nor night; that men may bring unto thee the wealth of the nations, and their kings led with them. . . . And the sons of them that afflicted thee shall come bending unto thee; and all they that despised thee shall bow themselves down at the soles of thy feet" (Is. 60 : 9–11, 14).

The guilt of the people and their punishment by God are buried in the past. No more thought is to be given to it. Again and again the prophet preaches that henceforth God will have nothing but compassion and love for Israel.

God will make a new covenant with his people and provide a descendant of David as ruler for them and for the whole world. "For the mountains shall depart, and the hills be removed; but my kindness shall not depart from thee, neither shall my covenant of peace be removed, saith the Lord that hath mercy on thee" (Is. 54 : 10). "I will make an everlasting covenant with you, even the sure mercies of David. Behold I have given him for a witness to the peoples, a leader and commander to the peoples" (Is. 55 : 3 f.). "And as for me, this is my covenant with them, saith the Lord: my spirit is upon thee, and my words which I have put in thy mouth, shall not depart out of thy mouth, nor out of the mouth of thy seed, nor out of the mouth of thy seed's seed, saith the Lord" (Is. 59 : 21).

Deutero-Isaiah (Is. 40–66): Ethical Monotheism

In the ethics preached by Deutero-Isaiah there breathes a new spirit. The earlier prophets were mainly concerned with the attitude which would be well-pleasing to God in the people as a whole, whereas Deutero-Isaiah is concerned with the attitude of the individuals who together make up the people of God's pleasure. It is an ethic which demands devotion to one's neighbours and praises humility. The ethics of Jesus are already being proclaimed. "To this man will I look, even to him that is poor and of a contrite spirit, and that trembleth at my word" (Is. 66 : 2). "Is not this the fast that I have chosen? To loose the bonds of wickedness, to undo the bands of the yoke, and to let the oppressed go free, and that ye break every yoke? Is it not to deal thy bread to the hungry, and that thou bring the poor that are cast out to thy house? When thou seest the naked, that thou cover him; and that thou hide not thyself from thine own flesh?" (Is. 58 : 6 f.).

The cultus has its place in Deutero-Isaiah, side by side with the ethics. True, he will not allow fasting to count as the right way to honour God, and it has no place in the new age. On the other hand, he attaches great importance to the proper hallowing of the Sabbath. He even regards the offering of sacrifices as pleasing to God. In the future whoever belongs to the people of Israel is to be called a priest of Yahweh (Is. 56 : 2; 60 : 7; 61 : 6).

In Deutero-Isaiah monotheism reaches its full development. It is no longer enough to look up to Yahweh as the God who is exalted far above the gods of other peoples by his power and his ethical nature. He moves on from the conception of his uniqueness, which is found in the earlier prophets, to that of his sole existence. For Deutero-Isaiah it is folly to attribute existence to gods fashioned by human hand. There is only one God. It is he who created heaven and earth. Everything is subject to him. All peoples belong to him, Israel in a special way as his people whom he has chosen for himself. That he is Lord of all peoples can be seen from the fact that Cyrus, the mighty King of the Persians, who does not know the true God, has to carry out what God has in mind for his people. "I am the Lord, and there is none else. I form the light, and create darkness; I make peace, and create evil" (Is. 45 : 6 f.).

Deutero-Isaiah (Is. 40–66): The Suffering Servant of God

Deutero-Isaiah is not completely satisfied with the explanation that God has scattered his people among the Gentiles and allowed them to suffer so grievously at their hands simply in order that he may take them back into his favour after they have been punished. He takes it for granted that what they have suffered must have some further meaning. This he finds in the fact that their dispersion among the Gentiles is intended to afford the latter the possibility of becoming acquainted with the true God. They are to profit by what the captives from God's people dwelling in their midst have endured at their hands. This second interpretation of the suffering allotted to the people eventually supersedes the first. Deutero-Isaiah sees it as higher and truer. He proclaims it as a mystery.

It is the will of Yahweh, according to him, that all peoples shall come to Jerusalem to honour God in his Temple. "My house shall be a house of prayer for all nations" (Is. 56 : 7). He will even accept some of the strangers who have become believers as priests (Is. 66 : 21).

The universalism which can first be observed in Jeremiah's eschatological expectation becomes the dominant note in Deutero-Isaiah.[1] The meditations on the suffering Servant of God (יהוה עבד Ebed Yahweh) are related to the redemption which the people of God have won for the Gentiles by allowing them to become acquainted with the true God. In these passages it is sometimes God, sometimes the people of Israel, and sometimes the Gentiles who speak about the sufferings of Israel as the Servant of God. Yahweh speaks to his people Israel: "It is too light a thing that thou shouldest be my servant to raise up the tribes of Jacob, and to restore the preserved of Israel: I will also give thee for a light to the Gentiles, that thou mayest be my salvation unto the end of the earth" (Is. 49 : 6). The people of Israel speaks: "The Lord God hath opened mine ear, and I was not rebellious, neither turned away backward. I gave my back to the smiters, and my cheeks to them that plucked off the hair: I hid not my face from shame and spitting. For the Lord God will help me" (Is. 50 : 5–7). The Gentiles speak: "He was despised, and rejected of men; a man of sorrows, and acquainted with grief. . . . Surely he hath borne our griefs, and carried our sorrows: yet we did esteem him stricken, smitten of God, and afflicted. But he was wounded for our transgressions, he was bruised for our iniquities: the chastisement of our peace was upon him; and with his stripes we are healed. All we like sheep have gone astray; we have turned every one to his own way; and the Lord hath laid on him the iniquity of us all" (Is. 53 : 3–6). Only the people of Israel can be meant

[1] The saying in Is. 2 : 1–4 about the Gentiles making pilgrimage to Jerusalem does not come from the eighth-century prophet Isaiah, but belongs to the same period as Deutero-Isaiah. Jeremiah is the first to express the idea that the Gentile nations are included by God within the compass of his grace.

by the suffering Servant of God. Everywhere in Deutero-Isaiah it is they who are addressed by God as his Servant.

There are, however, a few passages in which the interpretation of what is said with reference to the corporate personality of the people does present difficulties. We are tempted to assume that the reference is to an individual person, perhaps a martyred prophet of the time of the Exile. Nevertheless the attempt to take the Servant as representing an individual figure as well as the people cannot be sustained. In the continuation of the passage it always becomes plain that the reference is to the people. The difficulties in always recognizing the people of Israel in the suffering Servant derive from the fact that the writer of the songs goes so far in personifying the people that he speaks of the Servant as being called while he was still in his mother's womb (Is. 49 : 1) and of his death and burial (Is. 53 : 8 f.), as if he were speaking of a man.

Similarly in Is. 53 : 9 f. it is said of God's Servant that he has done no wrong and no lie will be found on his lips, and that he has freely sacrificed himself and freely borne the sufferings of many. We must not be misled by this into doubting that it is the people that is meant in this description. The passage is put forward as a reflection of the Gentiles on the wonderful meaning that the fate of Israel has for them. It is not for the Gentiles to consider that the people is at the same time doing penance for its own guilt and taking upon itself humiliation and suffering not of its own free will but under compulsion from God. To the Gentiles it looks as if it were by an act of free will that they have been granted the redemption that is now open to them. Here the original meaning of the people's suffering is not merely overlaid but replaced by the new, with its reference to the Gentiles.

In the last sections of the Book of Isaiah (which probably do not come from the real Deutero-Isaiah, the composer of Is. 40–62, but from a later prophet belonging to the end of the Exilic period) the theme is a new creation of heaven and earth. "For, behold, I create new heavens and a new earth: and the former things shall not be remembered" (Is. 65 : 17). "For as the new heavens and the new earth, which I will make, shall remain before me, saith the Lord, so shall your seed and your name remain" (Is. 66 : 22). Here the idea, found in Isaiah and Ezekiel, and further developed by Deutero-Isaiah, that a wonderful transformation of nature will take place in the age of the Kingdom of God, reaches its final conclusion. The Kingdom is beginning to become something wholly supernatural.

Jesus was familiar with the thought of Deutero-Isaiah. Without actually quoting him, he certainly has passages from him in mind.

3. THE KINGDOM OF GOD IN THE POST-EXILIC PROPHETS

Haggai and Zechariah

The return to Jerusalem took place in 538, but the intervention of God foretold by Deutero-Isaiah did not ensue. The people found difficulty in maintaining their position against the enemies they encountered in their homeland. The building of the new temple had to wait for a number of years after the laying of the foundation stone because the returning exiles would not allow any share in the sanctuary to the Israelites from the Northern Kingdom who had settled in Judaea. These immediately denounced them to the Persian court as seeking to re-establish the former independent Jewish state and procured a withdrawal of permission to continue the rebuilding of the Temple. This ban was not lifted until 520, the second year of Darius (521–486). The consecration of the new Temple eventually took place in 516. The prophets Haggai and Zechariah appeared in the year in which the building of the Temple was resumed. From them we learn that the people had as their leaders in this undertaking Zerubbabel, the governor of Judah and a descendant of David, and the high priest Joshua. They see in Zerubbabel the ruler of the coming Kingdom of Glory chosen by God.

Although the events following the return had followed such a mundane and melancholy course, the two prophets did not cease to expect the miracle of a speedy divine intervention. "For thus saith the Lord of hosts: Yet once, it is a little while, and I will shake the heavens, and the earth, and the sea, and the dry land; and I will shake all nations . . . and I will fill this house [the Temple] with glory" (Hag. 2 : 6 f.). "Speak to Zerubbabel, governor of Judah, saying, I will shake the heavens and the earth: and I will overthrow the throne of kingdoms, and I will destroy the strength of the kingdoms of the nations; . . . In that day, saith the Lord of hosts, will I take thee, O Zerubbabel, my servant, the son of Shealtiel, saith the Lord, and will make thee as a signet: for I have chosen thee" (Hag. 2 : 21–23). "Jerusalem shall be inhabited as villages without walls, by reason of the multitude of men and cattle therein. For I, saith the Lord, will be unto her a wall of fire round about, and I will be the glory in the midst of her" (Zech. 2 : 4 f.). "This is the word of the Lord unto Zerubbabel, saying, Not by might, nor by power, but by my spirit, saith the Lord of hosts. Who art thou, O great mountain? Before Zerubbabel thou shalt become a plain" (Zech. 4 : 6 f.). "Many peoples and strong nations shall come to seek the Lord of hosts in Jerusalem, and to intreat the favour of the Lord" (Zech. 8 : 22).

Malachi: The Return of Elijah

Once again all these hopes were doomed to disappointment. Nothing more is heard of Zerubbabel; there is no record of what became of him. How things stood in Jerusalem about 450 can be seen from the teaching of the prophet Malachi. He reproaches the priests with keeping the best animals for themselves and sacrificing only those with blemishes, and with forsaking altogether the right path. He makes it plain that among the ordinary people the sanctity of marriage was not being preserved, Jewish men were marrying Gentile women and God was cheated when the tithe was offered.

Accordingly the preaching of Malachi strikes a quite different note from that of Deutero-Isaiah, Haggai and Zechariah. There is no trace here of their exuberant hopefulness. He cannot promise, like them, that the judgement and punishing hand of God belong to the past and that only the Kingdom of Glory lies ahead. Once more, as in the days of Amos and Hosea and Isaiah, the Day of

Yahweh must be envisaged as a Day of Judgement even for his people.

What is new in Malachi is that God will send back to earth the prophet Elijah, who had been translated into his presence in heaven, to proclaim the great day and prepare men for it. "Behold, I send my messenger, and he shall prepare the way before me: and the Lord, whom ye seek, shall suddenly come to his temple; and the messenger of the covenant, whom ye delight in, behold, he cometh, saith the Lord of hosts. But who may abide the day of his coming? And who shall stand when he appeareth? . . . I will come near to you to judgement; and I will be a swift witness against the sorcerers, and against the adulterers, and against false swearers; and against those that oppress the hireling in his wages, the widow, and the fatherless, and that turn aside the stranger from his right, and fear not me" (Mal. 3 : 1 f., 5). "For, behold, the day cometh, it burneth as a furnace; and all the proud, and all that work wickedness, shall be stubble: and the day that cometh shall burn them up, saith the Lord of hosts, that it shall leave them neither root nor branch. But unto you that fear my name shall the sun of righteousness arise . . . And ye shall tread down the wicked" (Mal. 4 : 1–3). "Behold, I will send you Elijah the prophet before the great and terrible day of the Lord come. And he shall turn the heart of the fathers to the children, and the heart of the children to their fathers; lest I come and smite the earth with a curse" (Mal. 4 : 5 f.). Because the events are once more like those of the pre-Exilic age, Malachi and the prophets who follow him have to preach the coming of the Judgement and that of the Kingdom together, like the prophets of that earlier time.

Our knowledge of the historical events of this later post-Exilic period is very scanty. About 350 a large number of Jews were led off into captivity, probably because they had taken part in a rising against the Persians. When the Persian Empire broke up, Judaea became in 332 a province in the empire of Alexander the Great. After his death it suffered severely for a time in the wars fought between the Egyptian kings and the Seleucid rulers of Asia Minor with varying fortunes for its possession. There was a repetition of what had happened in the time of Isaiah and Jeremiah. In the course of these struggles, about 320 a number of Jews were carried off to Egypt. From 197 onwards the Seleucid kings were finally established as the masters of Palestine.

Joel; Isaiah 24–27; Zechariah 9–14

Of the prophets who followed Malachi, Joel and the anonymous writers of the passages which have come down to us as Isaiah 24–27 and Zechariah 9–14 are known to us. This second portion of the Book of Zechariah does not come from the prophet Zechariah, who appeared shortly after the return from the Exile. It is known as Deutero-Zechariah (the second Zechariah). Joel should be placed about 400. Isaiah 24–27 and Zechariah 9–14 probably belong to the period following the end of Persian rule in 332.

In Joel the picture of the future is brighter than in Malachi. He sees the meaning of the Day of Yahweh in God's protection of his people and vindication of them against the Gentile nations that mock and oppress them. In the Day of Yahweh everyone who calls upon his name will be saved. Judgement will be carried out on the Gentiles in the Valley of Jehoshaphat. An important feature of Joel's hope for the future is that the approach of the Day of Yahweh will be marked by the outpouring of the Spirit of God and by miracles. "And it shall come to pass afterward, that I will pour out my spirit upon all flesh; and your sons and your daughters shall prophesy, your old men shall dream dreams, your young men shall see visions: and also upon the servants and upon the handmaids in those days will I pour out my spirit. And I will show wonders in the heavens and in the earth, blood, and fire, and pillars of smoke. The sun shall be turned into darkness, and the moon into blood, before the great and terrible day of the Lord come" (Joel 2 : 28–31).

The eschatological expectation of the writer of Isaiah 24–27 is in general agreement with that of Joel. In this writer for the first time we find the punishment of heavenly beings who have fallen away from God playing a part in the description of the Day of

Yahweh. In his opinion they will eventually be forgiven. "And it shall come to pass in that day, that the Lord shall punish the host of the high ones on high, and the kings of the earth upon the earth. And they shall be gathered together, as prisoners are gathered in the pit, and shall be shut up in the prison, and after many days shall they be visited" (Is. 24 : 21 f.). The origin of the late Jewish concept of angelic beings who rebel against God is the myth of the sons of God who, according to Gen. 6 : 1-4, took the daughters of men to wife. The development of this idea took place under the influence of the Zoroastrian religion.

In Isaiah 24-27 we also hear for the first time of the miraculous meal which God prepares for those who have a place in his Kingdom, and of the great trumpet which will sound on the Day of Yahweh. "And in this mountain [Zion] shall the Lord of hosts make unto all peoples a feast of fat things, a feast of wines on the lees, of fat things full of marrow, of wines on the lees well refined" (Is. 25 : 6). "And it shall come to pass in that day, that a great trumpet shall be blown; and they shall come which were ready to perish in the land of Assyria, and they that were outcasts in the land of Egypt; and they shall worship the Lord in the holy mountain at Jerusalem" (Is. 27 : 13).

The section constituting Zechariah 9-14 contains, as does Isaiah 24-27, much that is obscure simply because there are frequent references to historical events unknown to us. Who is the figure spoken of when it is said that the inhabitants of Jerusalem "shall look unto me whom they have pierced: and they shall mourn for him, as one mourneth for his only son" (Zech. 12 : 10)? Who is meant by the worthless shepherd whom Yahweh puts in charge of his people and later rejects (Zech. 11 : 15-17 and 13 : 7-9)? The description of what happened to this shepherd underlies the saying of Jesus to his disciples on the way to Gethsemane: "I will smite the shepherd, and the sheep of the flock shall be scattered abroad" (Mt. 26 : 31; Zech. 13 : 7).

The writer of Zechariah 9-14 reveals his dependence on Ezekiel in the prophecy that the neighbourhood of Jerusalem will become level ground on the Day of Yahweh (Zech. 14 : 3-5, 10) and that from Jerusalem living water will flow into the Eastern and the Western seas (Zech. 14 : 8). Joel also shares Ezekiel's expectation that a spring will arise in the Temple and become a river (Joel 3 : 18).

Like all the post-exilic prophets, the writer of Zechariah 9-14 expects the Gentile nations, in so far as they have not been destroyed in the Day of Yahweh, to come to Jerusalem to pray to the true God. He assumes that they will go on doing this year after year. The way in which he pictures the destruction of the Gentile nations is that, among other calamities sent upon them by Yahweh, a great panic will fall upon them and they will rise up and slay one another (Zech. 14 : 13).

The Messianic Kingdom and the Kingdom of God

The disappointment of the hopes which Haggai and Zechariah had fixed upon Zerubbabel in the period just after the return from captivity and the utter failure to establish the Davidic Kingdom are an important factor in the formation of eschatological expectation.[2] The conception of the Kingdom as involving the reign of a Messiah of David's line, which goes back to Isaiah, recedes into the background. In Malachi and the post-Exilic prophets who follow him the Messianic king no longer plays any part. As in Amos and Hosea, their expectation is fixed on the Kingdom in which God will reign. Malachi, Joel and the author of Isaiah 24-27 make no mention at all of a descendant of David. In Deutero-Zechariah (Zech. 12 : 8-10 and 13 : 1) the House of David is named as occupying a place of honour before God, but there is no word of a future king of David's line.

In the period after the Exile the Kingdom of Judah was a theocracy. Consequently God himself alone comes under consideration as king in the Jerusalem of the future. "So shall ye know that I am the Lord your God, dwelling in Zion my holy mountain" (Joel 3 : 17). "For the Lord of hosts shall reign in mount Zion, and in Jerusalem" (Is. 24 : 23). "Every one that is left of all the nations which came against Jerusalem shall go up

[2] On the expectation of Haggai and Zechariah that Zerubbabel would be the Messiah, see p. 19f.

from year to year to worship the King, the Lord of hosts"
(Zech. 14 : 16). The Messianic Kingdom of the earlier prophets
and the Kingdom of God seen by the prophets of the later post-
Exilic age differ not only in that in the one the Messiah reigns,
in the other God himself. Their whole nature is different.

The Messianic Kingdom of Isaiah, Jeremiah, Ezekiel and
Deutero-Isaiah is a spiritual and ethical dimension. It arises through
the working of God's spirit in men: in the king descended from
David (in Isaiah), or in him and the whole people (in Jeremiah,
Ezekiel and Deutero-Isaiah).[3] These prophets anticipate that, in
the age of the Messianic Kingdom, not only will the ethical
replace the non-ethical, but there will also occur a more or less
widespread transformation of the natural into the supernatural.
This, however, makes no difference to the nature of the Kingdom.[4]
The operation of the Spirit of God working on men remains the
dominating factor. The previous transformation of nature is a
minor accompaniment. The spiritual and ethical character of the
Kingdom is preserved.

In Malachi, and in Joel and the writers of Isaiah 24–27 and
Zechariah 9–14, however, this is no longer true. In them the
Kingdom is supernatural in its very nature. It does not come in
the operation of God's Spirit in men, but appears as a ready-made
divine creation.

It is Daniel who draws out the consequences of the supernatural character of the expected Kingdom. Not only, like the
prophets of the later post-Exilic period, does he disregard the
Messianic king of David's line: he puts in his place the Son of Man,
a being whom God sends down from heaven to reign in the Kingdom.

4. THE KINGDOM OF GOD IN DANIEL

Prophets and Apocalyptists

The Book of Daniel is an apocalypse. An apocalypse (from the
Greek word apokalypsis, $\dot{\alpha}\pi o\varkappa\dot{\alpha}\lambda\upsilon\psi\iota\varsigma$, unveiling or revelation) is

[3] See p. 6 ff.
[4] On this transformation of nature in Isaiah, Ezekiel and Deutero-Isaiah,
see p. 7 ff.

a prophetic writing with the peculiar characteristic that its author does not publish it under his own name, but under that of some well-known religious personality of the past. The real prophet speaks to his contemporaries about the meaning that some historical event which they have both experienced has in relation to the coming of the Kingdom for which they are longing. He warns them, punishes them, consoles them. If he also sets down his preaching in written form, he does it in order that it may be preserved. The apocalyptist is not addressing his hearers but his readers. He is of necessity a writing prophet. Only as such can he appear in the rôle of a religious figure from the remote past prophesying for a later time.

In the classical apocalypse (such as we have in the Book of Daniel) the alleged writer undertakes to predict the course of history from his own day in the remote past to the age in which the real writer lives, as something glimpsed in a series of visions, and rounds it off with visions of the final age. Since the reader can establish the accuracy of the prophecies of past events, it is hoped that he will come to be convinced that the events still to come will occur as foreseen.

It is also characteristic of apocalypses that, as Daniel does, they attempt to determine the date of the appearance of the Kingdom. They lay down all that must occur in order that it may come. They are at pains to give a survey of the events which, according to the preaching of the earlier prophets, belong to the final age, and thus offer a doctrine of their course and succession.

Christian dogma invented for the doctrine of "the last things" the term eschatology (from the Greek words eschatos, ἔσχατος, the last, and logos, teaching). This term was adopted by theological scholars because it was so useful. They understand by eschatology the sum of the ideas which in different periods belong to Jewish and Christian expectation of the coming of the Kingdom of God.

Why does the author of the Book of Daniel (the first in Jewish prophetic literature to do so) write under an assumed name drawn from the past? The answer is, because in his day the collection of Old Testament writings, and so of the prophets, had already assumed a fixed form. Accordingly, Malachi counted as the last of the prophets. It was assumed that the prophetic gift was henceforth extinct. Only in the future was the possibility left open that prophets might reappear.

This is attested by the First Book of Maccabees for the age of the Maccabean Wars to which the Book of Daniel (completed about 165) belongs. When the altar of burnt offering in the Temple at Jerusalem was broken up because it had been desecrated by the offering on it of heathen sacrifice, no one knew what was the proper thing to do with the stones which had once been part of the sanctuary. They therefore resolved as a temporary measure to lay them up in "a convenient place on the Temple hill until there should come a prophet to tell what to do with them" (1 Macc. 4 : 46). In the same way, some time later Simon, the brother of Judas Maccabeus, was provisionally given the high priesthood as a hereditary office for his family, until a faithful prophet should arise, who would confirm or repudiate this descision on the basis of a revelation (1 Macc. 14 : 41).

Because of the dominant conviction that men were living in an age devoid of prophets, the writer of the Book of Daniel finds it appropriate to make his predictions, if they are to enjoy prophetic authority, appear to come from a religious figure of the past. The remarkable thing is that the falsity of this literary fiction, found in the Book of Daniel and later apocalypses, was not perceived in antiquity until well into the Christian era. Any mode of expression which seemed calculated to add authority to religious preaching regarded as valuable and necessary was held to be legitimate. Apocalyptic is an unnatural and often lifeless form of prophecy. But this does not mean that writings of this kind cannot have meaning and include valuable ideas.

Daniel's Apocalypse

The apocalyptist who writes under the pseudonym of Daniel lived at the time when the Seleucid King of Syria, Antiochus IV Epiphanes (175–164), was beginning to carry out his project of stamping out the Jewish religion and replacing it by Greek. In

the year 169 he pillaged the Temple at Jerusalem. He next
proceeded to forbid on pain of death observance of the Sabbath
and possession of the Law. He had the walls of Jerusalem torn
down, occupied the citadel with Syrian troops and demanded
that heathen sacrifices should be offered in all the cities of Judaea.
In December 168 he had an altar of Zeus erected over the great
altar of burnt offering in the Temple at Jerusalem. Upon this
there broke out in 167 a rising led by the priest Mattathias from
Modein and his five sons. The heathen altars in the land were
destroyed. In the course of the years 166 and 165 Judas Maccabeus,
the son of Mattathias, won a series of victories over the Syrian
troops. He won control of Jerusalem, though the citadel remained
untaken. In December 165 the Temple was reconsecrated. In
June 164 Antiochus Epiphanes died.

The writer of the Book of Daniel presupposes in his prophecies
the reconsecration of the Temple, but not the death of Antiochus.
He must therefore have completed the writing of his work
between December 165 and June 164. The purpose of the book
is to encourage the people to hold out in the fearful persecution
which they had to endure under Antiochus Epiphanes. It purports
to be written by the Jew Daniel, who came to Babylon as a boy
in the first captivity of 597, won Nebuchadnezzar's favour as a
page at his court, remained steadfast in all the persecutions he
had to endure because of his faith, was miraculously preserved
by God each time his life was in danger, and was still alive in the
third year of King Cyrus.

Daniel: The Events of the Final Age

In a series of visions present to his imagination of struggles
taking place between fierce beasts, Daniel looks ahead to struggles
in which four empires, the Babylonian, the Median, the Persian
and the Greek Empire of Alexander the Great follow one upon
the other. The last appears in the form of a he-goat, on whose
head eleven horns grow, one after another. These are the kingdoms that arose out of that of Alexander. The last and greatest

horn is that of Antiochus Epiphanes. In it are "eyes like the eyes of a man, and a mouth speaking great things" (Dan. 7 : 8).

From the succession of events preached by Daniel three hundred years earlier the people of God are meant to learn in a later time that the persecutions they have suffered under the blasphemer Antiochus Epiphanes mean the end of ordinary history and the beginning of a transcendent history. From this knowledge they are to acquire the strength to remain steadfast.

Daniel sees as events in which ordinary history gives place to supernatural the destruction of the beast which represents the kingdom of Antiochus Epiphanes and the handing over of the sovereignty in the Kingdom which follows it to a being whose form is like a son of man (whereas the representatives of the successive world empires have appeared in the form of animals). "I beheld till thrones were placed, and one that was ancient of days did sit: his raiment was white as snow, and the hair of his head like pure wool; his throne was fiery flames, and the wheels thereof burning fire. A fiery stream issued and came forth from before him: thousand thousands ministered unto him, and ten thousand times ten thousand stood before him: the judgement was set, and the books were opened. . . . I beheld even till the beast was slain, and his body destroyed, and he was given to be burned with fire, And as for the rest of the beasts, their dominion was taken away: yet their lives were prolonged for a season and a time. I saw in the night visions, and, behold, there came with the clouds of heaven one like unto a son of man, and he came even to the ancient of days, and they brought him near before him. And there was given him dominion, and glory, and a kingdom, that all the peoples, nations, and languages should serve him: his dominion is an everlasting dominion, which shall not pass away, and his kingdom that which shall not be destroyed" (Dan. 7 : 9–14). A great tribulation will precede the appearance of the Kingdom of God. At an appointed time the saints will be delivered into the power of the godless king who corresponds to the last horn (Dan. 7 : 25). "And at that time shall Michael stand up, the great prince which standeth for the children of thy people: and there shall be a time of trouble, such as never was since there was a nation even to that same time: and at that time thy people shall be delivered, every one that shall be found written in the book" (Dan. 12 : 1).

After the tribulation will come the judgement, the appearance of the Kingdom and the resurrection of the dead, in which Daniel will share. "But the judgement shall sit, and they shall take away his dominion [from the godless king], to consume and to destroy it unto the end. And the kingdom and the dominion, and the greatness of the kingdoms under the whole heaven, shall be given to the people of the saints of the Most High" (Dan. 7 : 26 f.). "And many of them that sleep in the dust of the earth shall awake, some to everlasting life, and some to shame and everlasting contempt. And they that be wise shall shine as the brightness of the firmament; and they that turn many to righteousness as the stars for ever and ever" (Dan. 12 : 2 f.). "But go thou [Daniel] thy way till the end be: for thou shalt rest, and shalt stand in thy lot, at the end of the days" (Dan. 12 : 13).

The explanation of the visions is given to Daniel by angelic beings in human form. Out of the great number of these there stand out archangels who are the guardian angels of the nations. Those who are called to the Kingdom are described not as righteous, but as saints, in the explanations which Daniel receives from the angels.

Daniel: The Son of Man

The expression Son of Man is not in itself a title of honour, but only refers to a human or manlike being. Ezekiel is addressed by God in his visions as Son of Man, and so is Daniel by the angel Gabriel (Dan. 8 : 17). With reference to Daniel's vision of the Son of Man who appears before God on the clouds of heaven, the term Son of Man became in the period which follows the title of the heaven-sent ruler in the Kingdom of God.

Why does Daniel abandon the view found in the later post-Exilic prophets that God himself is the ruler in the Kingdom? He does so because it is no longer compatible with his exalted view of the transcendence of God to see him enthroned in Jerusalem and ruling the nations. In his teaching God does not, in the period preceding the Kingdom, concern himself directly with the affairs of his people, but delegates these to the archangel Michael as his deputy.

Daniel is probably influenced also by the old prophetic concept of the Messiah who reigns in heaven on God's behalf. He cannot fully accept it, because for him the Kingdom is something entirely supernatural. The king of David's line, even if he is endowed with the Spirit of God, cannot reign over those who are in the position of having risen from the dead. The prophets of the late post-Exilic age gave up the concept of the Messiah as ruler of the Kingdom because the royal line of the House of David had ceased to exist and the concept of the Messiah was no longer compatible with that of the completely supernatural Kingdom. Daniel, however, makes the necessary change to correspond. He retains the idea of a human figure ruling as God's deputy, but for him this figure is no longer one born as a descendant of David, but is sent down from heaven.

A great deal in Daniel's conception of the Son of Man remains uncertain. What is the relation between the Son of Man, to whom God hands over sovereignty in the Kingdom, and the supernatural human figure who speaks with Daniel in the vision in the tenth chapter and then leaves him to join the archangel Michael and fight against the guardian angels of the Persian and Greek Empires (Dan. 10 : 16–21)? They can hardly be identical, since the activity of the former begins only with the appearance of the King-dom.

Nor is the origin of the Son of Man altogether clear. He does not seem to belong to the usual circle around God. He does, indeed, come proceeding on the clouds of heaven, and it is God who brings him. But is the generally accepted view that in Daniel he is a pre-existent being, who has always, like the angels, had his home in the heavenly regions, so absolutely certain? Is it im-possible that Daniel conceives him as a man who will be exalted to heaven at the end of time and will appear from there to reign in the Kingdom, endowed with the supernatural power that is there conferred upon him?

The Resurrection of the Dead

The only mention of resurrection of the dead prior to Daniel is in the section Isaiah 24–27, which probably originated in the period following 300. "He hath swallowed up death for ever" (Is. 25 : 8). "Thy dead shall live; my dead bodies shall arise. Awake and sing, ye that dwell in the dust: for thy dew is as the dew of herbs, and the earth shall cast forth the dead" (Is. 26 : 19). It is hard for us to believe that the earlier prophets do not take a resurrection of the dead for granted. How could they fail to be conscious of a problem, when those who had striven to become righteous and well-pleasing to God in hopes of the Kingdom could have no prospect of attaining it unless its coming took place in the lifetime of their generation? Yet it is indeed so. The prophets are concerned with the people as a whole and its future in such a way that it never occurs to them to consider the problem raised by the fate of the individual. Ezekiel, indeed, does begin to attend to this question. He assumes that those who survive the destruction of Jerusalem by the Chaldaeans in 586 owe this to the protection that God accords to them as the pious (Ezk. 9 : 3–6; 14 : 21 f.; 18 : 5–9).[5]

His view that those who are to be protected are specially marked and that certain names are written down in the Book of Life is taken over by the post-Exilic prophets. It applies, however, only to salvation during their lifetime, not to one available at the resurrection to judgement. Ezekiel's vision of the bones which become alive again (Ezk. 37 : 1–14) does not refer to the resurrection of individuals, but to the reconstitution of Israel from the remnant of the people which remains after the visitation.

Though frequently proclaimed by the prophets as imminent, the coming of the Kingdom was constantly deferred. In the course of time the thought must have forced itself upon their minds that there was a problem here. As age succeeded age, more and more of the righteous were being deprived of participation in the Kingdom as their generation passed away. If belief in the Kingdom was to remain strong, there must be an accompanying belief

[5] See also p. 12.

in the resurrection which would take place at the coming of the Kingdom.

Daniel takes it for granted that pious and godless will rise together, the pious to a blessed existence in the Kingdom of God, the others to one of damnation. He does not seem to conceive of a destruction of all the godless at the end of time.

The idea of resurrection was never universally accepted in late Judaism. The scribes who came from Pharisaic circles adopted it. The Sadducees, on the other hand, rejected it as an innovation. They adhered to the expectation of the older prophets, as if the old pre-individualistic point of view could still be maintained. They also refused to adopt the concept of a variety of angelic beings, which is found in Daniel. Since the preaching of Jesus takes the resurrection of the dead for granted, the Sadducees set him a question which would show that it was unimaginable. They present the case of seven men who had married the same wife, dying one after another, and want to know which of them will have her as his wife at the resurrection. He tells them that for those who are risen there will be no more marrying and being given in marriage, since they are "like angels in heaven" (Mt. 22 : 23–30).

5. JEWISH AND IRANIAN BELIEF IN THE KINGDOM OF GOD

Zarathustra as Reformer of the Iranian Religion

Belief in the resurrection came into Jewish eschatological expectation under the influence of the religion of Zarathustra. One thing which this Aryan-Iranian religion has in common with Semitic-Jewish is that in both the idea of the Kingdom of God stands at the centre of the faith.

Zarathustra, the reformer of the Iranian religion, probably appeared between 650 and 600. Iran, the land of the Aryans, is the name given in antiquity to the region which stretches east from the Tigris towards India between the Caspian Sea on the north and the ocean on the south. Between 1000 and 900 B.C.

Aryan tribes from the neighbourhood of the Pamir highlands migrated into it. The Medes and Persians settled in the west. Separated from them by the great salt desert, the Eastern Iranians occupied Bactria (the present Afghanistan) and the district south of it (now Beluchistan).

Zarathustra appeared in Bactria. In Eastern Iran cultural influences from the West (Mesopotamia and Asia Minor) had not yet made the same impact as in Media and Persia. The population was just on the point of changing over from a nomadic to an agricultural way of life. This is the state of affairs implied in Zarathustra's reform of the old Iranian religion.

With Zarathustra the Eastern Iranian religion rises at one stroke from a primitive polytheism to ethical monotheism. The starting-point of his thought is the struggle between good and evil, which is being played out before his eyes between the tribes which still remain in the nomadic state and those which have gone over to agriculture and stock-raising. The new way of life demands ethical qualities: industry, respect for property, honesty, truthfulness, trustworthiness, a sympathetic relationship with the domestic animals. Inhabiting a common area with agricultural tribes, the nomads turned into brigands. They lived by attacking and robbing those who were raising herds and wresting its fruits from the grudging earth.

In this struggle between good and evil Zarathustra sees a manifestation of the principle which is at work throughout history in the conflict between a good and an evil power. The good is for him the god Ahura-Mazdāh, in whom he recognizes the creator of the world and the only true God. For him the previous gods have ceased to exist as such. In so far as they are on the side of the good, they become heavenly beings standing beside Ahura-Mazdāh. Those who enjoy reverence from the nomadic bandits counts as daēvas, evil demons dwelling in the steppes and deserts. Behind the word daēva lies the Indo-Germanic root of the Latin deus (god), which shows that we are dealing with former gods. Ahura is the general designation of an ethical divine being, Mazdāh is his name.

Modern scholars assume that in the West (i.e. in Media and

Persia) the division of the gods of Iranian polytheism into higher, good gods (ahuras) and lower, evil ones (daēvas) had already begun before Zarathustra. So too had the acceptance of Ahura-Mazdāh as the highest in the former group. In the Behistun inscription Darius I (522-486) calls himself a worshipper of Ahura-Mazdāh, without making any reference to Zarathustra and his religion. For him, however, this god was probably only the highest among the ahuras, not the only God. Zarathustra was the first to rise to monotheism.

The collection of sacred writings of the religion of Zarathustra is known as the Avesta. The Gāthās, in which some authentic speeches of the prophet himself are contained, belong to the oldest portions. Avesta means knowledge. The Gāthās are found in chapters 28-34, 43-51 and 53 of the Yasna, one of the books of the Avesta.

In the Gāthās Zarathustra describes how he was called by Ahura-Mazdāh to preach the true faith and combat the lie and wickedness. In one passage of the Yasna, belonging, like the Gāthās, to the oldest part of the Avesta, we find the creed of the true religion: "I scorn to be a worshipper of the daēvas, I acknowledge myself as a devotee of Mazdāh, a follower of Zarathustra . . . , a devotee of the immortal holy ones [i.e. the amesha spentas, the highest heavenly beings]. I swear to renounce stealing and the theft of cattle, the pillage and destruction of the villages of the worshippers of Mazdāh. I promise those who live in houses freedom of movement and dwelling, together with the domestic animals with whom they live on earth. I pledge myself to good thoughts, good words, good work" (Yasna 12 : 1-9).

The God of light has, according to Zarathustra, for his allies in the struggle which he wages with the powers of darkness, the heavenly beings surrounding him and those men who have committed themselves to the side of the good.

The opposition between good and evil, light and darkness, pervades the whole of existence. Certain animals, especially the domestic animals, belong to the good world. The dog and the ox are creatures of unqualified sanctity. Snakes, scorpions, frogs, toads and ants are considered to be in league with the evil powers.

Fire is sacred, as an element of life and purity. The reverence shown to it plays an important part in worship.

History is interpreted as meaning that evil will be completely subdued, and the world is developing towards the Kingdom, in which everything will happen in accordance with the will of the one ethical God. The idea of the realization of the Kingdom of God, like monotheism, first came into Iranian religion through Zarathustra. Every effort in the direction of the victory of good contributes to the decline of evil and the advancement of the Kingdom of God. This advance takes place wherever a believer builds a house, maintains a priest and a wife and child, rears domestic animals and herds, works and waters the soil.

Because the ethics of Zarathustra demand all that serves the realization of the Kingdom of God, they are characterized by a note of enthusiasm. A noteworthy feature is the importance attached, along with active zeal for good, to humility and the renunciation of anger. Compassion is demanded of the believer, so far as the duty of combating evil permits. He must, however, proceed to show relentless hostility to every being belonging to the world of evil, be it man or beast. There is no place for love in the religion of Zarathustra. One of the demands lying closest to his heart is the abolition of sacrifices requiring bloodshed. He bases it on pity for the poor sacrificial animals, but was unable to effect it. In later worship, sacrifices again find their place.

The end of the struggle which is being played out in the world will be that the powers of evil together with all the beings who belong to them will be overcome and judgement will be executed upon them. Zarathustra seems to have expected this consummation to take place in the near future. The coming of the new world recedes more and more into the distance in the faith of later generations.

This higher form of the Iranian religion which had arisen in Bactria came to Persia and Media because the Eastern Iranian districts came to form part of the great Persian Empire. As a result of the growth into a great empire, stretching from the Aegean Sea to India, the religion became known to the peoples of Asia Minor, Mesopotamia and Syria. It retained its influence even after the destruction of the Persian Empire by Alexander the Great. In the course of the development undergone by the religion of Zarathustra, the dualism and the doctrine of heavenly beings were still further elaborated. The heavenly court by which God is surrounded grew in numbers and variety. The evil powers found a prince in the person of Angra-Mainyu (Ahriman).

The death and extinction of human beings came to be thought of as the work of a demon. His destruction brings in the resurrection. The picture that came to be formed of the events of the final age was that at the end of time a redeemer figure will snatch control of the world from Ahriman, just when he seems to be winning the final struggle. An interesting feature is that this redeemer does not belong to the heavenly powers surrounding God, but comes into existence on earth.

The Influence of the Iranian on the Jewish Belief in the Kingdom of God

The most important influence which Iranian religion, as developed by Zarathustra, exercised on Jewish eschatological expectation consists in the stimulus it gave to the adoption of the indispensable idea of resurrection as a prelude to participation in the Kingdom of God. Strangely enough, the religion of Zarathustra includes side by side two different conceptions of life after death. According to one, the soul of the righteous man who has died crosses the Cinvat Bridge into the heaven of Ahura-Mazdāh, there to enjoy the food and drink of immortality. The evildoer may not cross the Bridge and enters into the home of the Lie, where he suffers torment. In the other view, the dead all rise together at the end of the world. The existence of these two doctrines side by side is probably due to the appearance of a new view alongside an older one, which it has not succeeded in completely displacing. The later doctrine is doubtless that of the universal bodily resurrection at the end of the world. It belongs to the expectation of a Kingdom of God, which came into Iranian religion only with Zarathustra.

There is a way in which the two views can be brought into harmony. It can be done if we suppose that the souls of the dead at first survive in a form of temporary existence (a happy one for the righteous, one of torment for the wicked), and then, when they have been reunited with the body at the resurrection, which takes place at the time when the Kingdom arrives, pass into a state of eternal blessedness or damnation. There is no such idea of a temporary continuance of existence after death in Isaiah 24–27 and in Daniel. Those who die remain dead until the resurrection. They are corpses "asleep in the dust".

Another idea which arose in Jewish eschatological expectation probably under the influence of Zoroastrianism is that of the destruction of the wicked by fire. In Zoroastrianism, however, it is only the demons who are destroyed by fire. According to a view already found in the Gāthās, men are delivered to the fire in order to undergo God's judgement and be shown to be righteous. "I will speak of the test which thou [Ahura-Mazdāh] wilt institute in order to demonstrate by the red fire guilt and merit . . . to set a mark by molten metal on the conscience, to the cost of false believers and to the profit of true believers" (Yasna 51 : 8).

In the religion of Zarathustra the final damnation at the Judgement is often replaced by a sentence of refining punishment which will one day have an end. The notion of Purgatory probably has its roots in Zoroastrianism. When it is assumed in Is. 24 : 21 f. that "the host of the high ones on high, and the kings of the earth upon the earth" will be imprisoned in a pit for punishment on the Day of Judgement, to receive after a long interval a visitation of grace, this corresponds to the outlook of Zoroastrianism.

A Zoroastrian touch in Daniel is the assumption that God is surrounded by a great host of heavenly beings, some of whom stand out as occupying the highest position. The archangels in Daniel correspond to the seven amesha spentas (the immortal ones who bring blessing). The view expressed in Is. 25 : 8 that at the time of the last Judgement God will swallow up death, thought of as a personal being, for ever probably goes back to the Zoroastrian notion of the demon responsible for death. The monster serpent Leviathan, whom God "will punish with his

sore and great and strong sword" on the Day of Judgement
(Is. 27 : 1) seems to come from Babylonian mythology.

Characteristics of the Iranian and the Jewish Belief in the Kingdom of God

The religion of Zarathustra did not influence the essential
nature of the Jewish expectation for the future. The Jewish and
Iranian beliefs in the Kingdom of God are certainly closely
related. At the same time each has its own special characteristics
in which it persists. The kinship rests on the fact that both religions
have in common an ethical and religious attitude which affirms
life and the world. This kind of outlook is bound to expect and
hope for a final development of man and the world determined
by God. The difference between them arises from the circumstances in which belief in the Kingdom of God has developed in
the two religions. In Judaism it arose (more than a century before
Zarathustra appeared) out of the traditional conception of
Yahweh's Day of Judgement.[6] With Zarathustra it is the creation
of a religious thinker. In Judaism it arises in a people which has
already achieved a certain material and spiritual civilization.
Zarathustra is confronted with the task of encouraging a nation of
tribesmen to change over from an amoral nomadic existence to
a settled one, with its implication of an ethical way of life and its
aspirations towards civilization. In Judaism the concern is with
interpreting historical events with reference to the coming of the
Kingdom. Zarathustra ignores history as it is actually taking
place, and is only concerned with his conception of history. He
dictates to history, in so far as he is seeking to bring about a
civilization which will lead to the Kingdom of God. He is setting
himself to bring into operation the struggle for the Kingdom.

The Jewish faith does not expect man to be God's ally. It
remains expectant. Its religious thought does not concern itself
with cultural progress. In Zarathustra (and in the purified form of
the Iranian religion which already existed before his time in

[6] See p. 3 ff.

Media and Persia) we find a bent for material and spiritual progress such as had never previously existed. Because the Persian Empire incorporated something of this spirit, it was quite different from the Assyrian and Babylonian Empires that had preceded it. How great Cyrus is, just in the magnanimity he shows in his treatment of the peoples subject to his rule! How important are the achievements of Darius and Xerxes in their effort to create a condition of order and prosperity in their Empire! Not until modern times, in the seventeenth and eighteenth centuries, is there an ethical pursuit of progress comparable to that of the Iranians.

The Meaning of the Dualism of Zarathustra for Graeco-Oriental Thought

The novel, and indeed indispensable, intellectual contribution of Zarathustra to the ancient world was ignored. It remained ineffectual. What was effectual was his dualism. This was accepted, and played for centuries an important part in the cultural history of the Graeco-Oriental world.

In the course of time Zarathustra's dualism became detached from his religion and from the enthusiastic determination with which it had been associated. Losing its original associations and becoming quite general, it declined into a spirit of life- and world-denial. In this form it became, towards the end of the pre-Christian era, an element in the spiritual life of Graeco-Oriental man. Through its influence the drive towards affirmation of life and the world became suspect. A mood of pessimistic brooding over the opposition of light and darkness, good and evil, perfection and imperfection, set in, which deprived men of their natural vigour. It led them to concern themselves exclusively with the problem of the imprisonment of the spirit in matter instead of how it could overcome matter.

This is what gave rise to the atmosphere in which Gnosticism, Neo-Pythagoreanism and Manicheism appeared. The Graeco-Oriental world absorbed the most dangerous element in Zarathustra's thought, and not the great side, in which he was far in advance of his age. The paradox ensues that he, of all men, should have contributed to an age of decadence.

In Persia his religion persisted for centuries. From the blazing fire which had once burst out, it became a tiny flame, laboriously preserved in the current dogmas and ceremonies. Despite the opportunity which the extensiveness of the Persian Empire had offered, the religion of Zarathustra was never to become the world religion that it might have been. With the fall of the Neo-Persian Sassanid kingdom in A.D. 640 it disappeared from the stage of history. It was unable to hold its own against Islam among a people subject to the Arabs. Indeed, Christianity also died out in the lands lost at this time to the Arabs.

A Gnostic religion, preaching redemption through negation of life and the world, was introduced by Mani in A.D. 242 and purported to be the true religion of Zarathustra. For a time this did become a world religion. In Asia it spread to India and China. In the West it appeared in the Roman Empire and claimed to be the true Christianity. Because of the number and importance of its adherents (Augustine was a Manichee for a time) it presented a real danger to the existence of the Christian church in the fourth century. As the official state church, the latter succeeded in invoking the help of the emperors against the heresy and, not without difficulty, in breaking the power of its rival in the course of the fifth century.

6. THE EXPECTATION OF THE KINGDOM OF GOD IN LATE JUDAISM

Late Judaism. The Apocalypses of Enoch, Baruch and Ezra.
The Psalms of Solomon

The age which is designated Late Judaism begins with Daniel. It lasts into the decades after the destruction of Jerusalem by Titus (A.D. 70). It is followed by the legal scholasticism of the Rabbis. This no longer produced writings with any kind of independent views on religious questions.

Three of the four works to which we owe our knowledge of the eschatological expectation of late Judaism are apocalypses. They purport to come from Enoch, Baruch and Ezra. The fourth is called the Psalms of Solomon. This collection makes no claim anywhere in the text to come from Solomon. Like Deutero-Isaiah, it consists of psalm-like songs of an unknown writer. They arose shortly after the capture of Jerusalem by Pompeius (64 B.C.). It is therefore probable that it was only later that they were ascribed to Solomon, because by this time no one could conceive of a psalmist as living at any time except the past. This collection of songs is not an apocalypse, but was later turned into one. These four books were not, like the Book of Daniel, able to win acceptance in the collection of the canonical scriptures. They retain their place among the apocryphal writings (i.e. among the sacred writings of the second rank), and so enjoy a position of some respect in Christianity as well as Judaism.

These four late Jewish writings have one thing in common. They do not expect the coming of the Kingdom to follow upon some particular historical event, as Daniel did when he saw the desecration of the Temple by Antiochus Epiphanes as a sign of the end of ordinary history. True, they too are moved by historical occurrences to look out for the events of the final era and form a picture of it. But they give up the claim to be able to say anything more precise about the time when these will take place. What is new is that for them the coming of the time of the Kingdom of God depends upon conditions which must first be fulfilled in accordance with God's will.

The Apocalypse of Enoch and the Psalms of Solomon both belong to the last century B.C. They are not, however, in agreement about the events of the final era. The Apocalypse of Enoch adheres to the view of the Book of Daniel, according to which the Son of Man is the ruler appointed by God over the Kingdom, which is thought of in purely supernatural terms. The Psalms of Solomon, on the other hand, look for the Kingdom of the Messiah of David's line.

One cannot understand the mood that prevails in the Book of Enoch unless one is familiar with the experiences of the party of the pious (Chassidim) in Judaea from the end of the second century B.C. to the capture of Jerusalem by Pompeius. The pious, who were strict in their loyalty to traditional religion and the Law, joined with the Maccabees in the struggle for the liberation of Judaea from the rule of the Seleucid kings of Syria. In 142 B.C. the latter surrendered the citadel at Jerusalem to Simon, the brother of Judas Maccabeus, and acknowledged the independence of Judaea. In the following year Simon was chosen by the people to be hereditary High Priest and at the same time Commander-in-Chief and Prince of Judaea, and he was recognized by the Romans as an ally (1 Macc. 14 : 24–49). The reign of the Hasmonean family began with him; it was named after his great-great-grandfather, Hasmoneus. Towards the end of the reign of his son John Hyrcanus I (135–105), however, there was a breach between him and the pious. From this time on the Hasmonean princes supported the hellenizing priestly families of the House of Zadok, who had been chief priest in Jerusalem under David. Because of their ancestry they are called Sadducees. The name Pharisees (separated) now came into use for the pious. They persisted in their opposition to the Hasmonean princes and the Sadducees. As the guardians of religion they enjoyed great respect from the people.

Under Alexander Jannaeus (104–78), the son of John Hyrcanus, the Pharisees underwent severe persecution because they would not recognize him as High Priest on account of his depraved living. After enjoying some years of peace under the woman who succeeded him, Alexandra (78–69 B.C.), they were again persecuted under Aristobulus II (66–63). In the Apocalypse of Enoch and the Psalms of Solomon we find the pious in the Pharisaic circle looking forward, in the midst of grave affliction, to the Kingdom of God.

The Apocalypses of Enoch, Baruch and Ezra have not been preserved in Hebrew, the language in which they were written, nor in the Greek translation which was made later. We possess them only in other languages. The reason for this remarkable fact is that the Jewish scribes who devoted themselves to rabbinical scholasticism in the period after the destruction of Jerusalem by Titus would have nothing to do with either apocalypses or works in Greek.[7]

Though no longer esteemed in Judaism, these writings now enjoyed high respect among Christians, and this saved them for a time, in the Greek translation, from disappearing altogether. Later they again came into danger. The scholarly theologians of the Greek church rejected them because they were offended by the fantastic and mythological notions that they found in them. So to a large extent the Greek translations also were lost, and they were preserved only in copies made in churches where Greek was not spoken, in Latin or Syriac or Ethiopic or Armenian. These sacred writings of the second rank owe a great deal to the Roman Catholic Church. This holds them in honour because it found many of its doctrines, for instance the value of good works, contained in them. The Council of Trent (1545–1563) even decreed that all the apocryphal writings contained in the Vulgate should enjoy the same respect as the canonical scriptures. The Jewish religion has received a valuable gift from Christianity in the preservation of these precious documents of late Jewish piety which it had allowed to become lost.

The Apocalypse of Enoch

Enoch is the seventh patriarch of the period before the Flood. Because of his piety he was taken into heaven without having to undergo death (Gen. 5 : 24), like the prophet Elijah later. The book that bears his name is a large work, preserved only in the translation made from Greek into Ethiopic. The Epistle of Jude (Jude 14 f.) quotes a passage from Enoch (En. 1 : 9) about the judgement which God, surrounded by myriads of saints, will execute upon the ungodly. The book was highly esteemed by the earlier church Fathers. Tertullian (d. 230) wanted to have it counted as one of the canonical writings of the New Testament. Later it lost its high reputation and fell more and more into neglect.

[7] Hermann Gunkel deals with the question of the fortunes of these writings in his masterly Introduction to the Apocalypse of Ezra in Kautzsch's German edition of The Apocrypha and Pseudepigrapha of the Old Testament.

Most of the Book of Enoch belongs to the first half of the first century B.C. It contains, however, some passages that are older still, dating from the end of the second century. In Enoch, as in Daniel, the writer is supposed to have had visions which give a survey of the events of world history as it approached the time of the end. The most important part of the book consists of the so-called Similitudes of Enoch (En. 37–69). These are explanations of the visions of the final events.[8] Enoch presupposes and expands the eschatological expectation of the Book of Daniel.

The situation in the world before the coming of the final events is described as follows. The fallen angels, who in union with the daughters of men created giants, "whereby the whole earth became full of blood and unrighteousness" (En. 9 : 9), are kept prisoner in a pit over which fire blazes until the judgement which will be executed upon them at the end of the world (En. 18 : 11–19 : 3).[9] The stars, which were disobedient to God and did not appear at the appointed time, will share their fate (En. 21 : 1–10). The fallen angels ask Enoch to draw up and present to God a petition begging for mercy upon them. In a vision he learns that this will not be granted (En. 13–16). The spirits of the dead have their abode in the Western regions of the underworld. The souls of the righteous dwell in a special place with a bright spring of water, and those of the pious "who were slain in the days of the sinners" are in another place, and those of the ungodly in yet another (En. 22 : 8–14).[10] According to Enoch the fate of the righteous dead is to be preferred to that of those who are still alive when they experience the coming of the Kingdom. He finds it written over them on "heavenly tablets" (En. 103 : 2 f.). We may infer from the fact that the spirits of the martyrs await the end of the times not with the righteous, but in a special place of their own (En. 22 : 12), that they have a place of honour

[8] Chapters 70 and 71, in which Enoch is made Son of Man on his translation to heaven, do not belong to the original contents of the book.

[9] The fall of the angels is recorded in Gen. 6 : 1–4. See p. 23.

[10] The idea that the dead do not rest in the grave, but that their souls await the final judgement in different places, according to whether they belonged to the good or the bad, comes from Zoroastrianism. See p. 38.

in the Kingdom. The punishment awaiting the spirits of the wicked is that they will go to a region of darkness, chains and blazing flames, where they will know no peace for all eternity (En. 103 : 8). The Satans appear before God to accuse men. They are kept in check by Phanuel, one of the four angels of the presence who constantly stand before the throne of God (En. 40 : 7). We find a similar view already expressed in the prophet Zechariah about 520 B.C. Here Satan appears as the accuser of the High Priest Joshua (Zech. 3 : 1 f.).

In a speech in which Enoch warns men to walk in the path of righteousness, woes are uttered against the rich. It is taken for granted that wealth can be acquired only by wickedness. "Woe to you rich, for you have relied on your riches . . . and not remembered the Most High. You have committed blasphemy and unrighteousness and have become ready for . . . the day of the great judgement. . . . For your fall there shall be no compassion" (En. 94 : 8–10).

The natural course of the world will continue "till the number of the righteous has been filled". Not until there are a fixed number of righteous ones and martyrs can God hearken to the prayer of the spirits of the pious who have died "that the postponement of their judgement may not last for ever" (En. 47 : 1–4).

Enoch: The Events of the Final Age. The Son of Man

For Enoch, as for Ezekiel and Daniel, the beginning of the final events is the raising of the great rebellion. In place of Gog and Magog, who in Ezekiel (Ezk. 38–39) attack Jerusalem from the north, we find in Enoch the Parthians and Medes, since in the last century B.C. these are the great threat to the Middle East. It is God who brings in the tribulation, by sending his angels to stir up the kings of the East to the wickedness of marching against Jerusalem. All that constitutes the final tribulation will come to pass in connexion with their coming. The destruction of these nations will take the form that they will be blinded by God and will kill one another (En. 56 : 5–7).

As in Joel (Joel 2 : 2 f.), at the time of the Judgement miracles will occur on earth and in heaven. The rain will be held back, the moon will "change her order and not appear at her time", and so will many of the stars (En. 80 : 2–7). A new feature in Enoch's description of the final tribulation is that kinsmen will attack one another in senseless rage. "A man shall not withhold his hand from slaying his sons and his sons' sons, and the sinner shall not withhold his hand from his honoured brother: from dawn till sunset they shall slay one another" (En. 100 : 2).

God appoints, according to Enoch, over the righteous of the final generation "holy angels to be their guardians, to guard them as the apple of an eye, until he has made an end of all wickedness and all sin" (En. 100 : 5). They are to remain alive for the coming of the Kingdom of God. Ezekiel's theory of their preservation remains in force even in the eschatology which stems from Daniel. What is new is the part that the angels play in the final tribulation.

When this final tribulation has lasted for its appointed time, the resurrection of the dead, the appearance of the Son of Man and the Judgement will take place. Enoch is aware that in Daniel the Son of Man is not a heavenly being belonging to God's entourage. He assumes that he has always existed but has remained hidden until the time when he comes forward. "Yea, before the sun and the signs [of the Zodiac] were created, before the stars of the heaven were made, his name was named before the Lord of spirits. He shall be a staff to the righteous and the saints whereon to stay themselves and not fall, and he shall be the light of the Gentiles and the hope of those who are troubled of heart. For this reason has he been chosen and hidden before him [God] before the creation of the world and he will be before him for evermore" (En. 48 : 3–6).

Whereas in Daniel God conducts the Last Judgement and the Son of Man then enters upon his reign over the Kingdom, in Enoch God also delegates the Judgement to him.[11] "And in those days shall the earth give back that which has been gathered

[11] This view is found in the majority of passages. In certain others God is the judge. The reason why in the Book of Enoch we find different ideas about the Judgement and other matters side by side is that passages of different origin are all included in it together.

together in it and Sheol also shall give back that which it has received. . . . The Elect One shall in those days sit on my throne and his mouth shall pour forth all the secrets of wisdom and counsel: for the Lord of spirits has given them to him" (En. 51 : 1–3). "And he [the Son of Man] sat on the throne of his glory, and the sum of judgement was given unto the Son of Man, and he caused the sinners to pass away and be destroyed from off the face of the earth and those who have led the world astray" (En. 69 : 27). "The righteous and elect shall be saved on that day. . . . And the Lord of spirits will abide over them and with that Son of Man shall they eat and lie down and rise up for ever and ever" (En. 62 : 13 f.). "All the righteous shall be angels in heaven" (En. 51 : 4). "Punishing angels will cast the kings and the mighty ones of the earth into the burning fire in a deep valley" (En. 54 : 1 f.). The same judgement is executed on the fallen angels by four archangels (Michael, Gabriel, Raphael and Phanuel: En. 54 : 6).

Enoch: Salvation through Repentance on the Day of Judgement. The Bestowal of Divine Wisdom

Enoch allows sinners a chance of still winning salvation through repentance made only on the actual Day of Judgement. "On the day of affliction evil shall have been treasured up against the sinners. And the righteous shall be victorious in the name of the Lord of spirits: and he will cause the others to witness this, that they may repent and forgo the works of their hands. They shall have no honour through the name of the Lord of spirits, yet through his name shall they be saved.[12] And the Lord of spirits will have compassion on them, for his compassion is great" (En. 50 : 2 f.). These recipients of grace at the last minute, who will "have no honour from the Lord of spirits", are the least in the Kingdom of heaven. The martyrs who rise at the resurrection will be among the greatest.[13]

[12] The theory that everyone who calls on the name of the Lord on the last day will be saved goes back to Joel 2 : 32.

[13] See p. 45f.

The end will be that God will create a new heaven and a new earth. This idea comes from Deutero-Isaiah. "I will transform the earth and make it a blessing: and I will cause my elect ones to dwell upon it" (En. 45 : 4 f.). The heavenly Jerusalem has its place in the new earth (En. 90 : 29-36).

Whereas in Jeremiah and Ezekiel God writes his law and implants his Spirit in the heart of those who have a place in the Kingdom, in Enoch they partake of God's wisdom, thought of as a heavenly being. The notion of wisdom as a divine being first appears in the type of Judaism which is becoming acquainted with Hellenism. It arises under the influence of the conception of world reason (*nous*), which is an element in Greek thought from the time of Anaxagoras (c. 500-428). Out of it developed the Stoic concept of the *logos*. The Jewish view of wisdom as a divine being first occurs in the collection of proverbs which came to be accepted in the canon of sacred scriptures under the title of the Proverbs of Solomon. "The Lord possessed me in the beginning of his way, before his works of old. I was set up from everlasting. . . . When there were no depths, I was brought forth. . . . When he established the heavens, I was there. . . . When he made firm the skies above. . . . When he gave to the sea its bound. . . . Then I was by him, as a master workman" (Prov. 8 : 22-30).

In the Book of the Proverbs of Jesus ben Sirach, which was probably composed between 190 and 170, and is thus a century older than the Book of Enoch, wisdom has her seat in God's sanctuary at Jerusalem. "I came forth from the mouth of the Most High, and covered the earth as a mist. I dwelt in high places, and my throne is in the pillar of the cloud. . . . He that created me made my tabernacle to rest. . . . In the holy tabernacle I ministered before him; and so was I established in Sion" (Ecclus. 24 : 3, 4, 8, 10).

What is special to Enoch is that the seat of wisdom is in heaven and its operation does not begin until the coming of the Kingdom. "When wisdom came to make her dwelling among the children of men, and found no dwelling-place, she returned to her place and took her seat among the angels" (En. 42 : 2). "Wisdom is poured out like water. . . . The Elect One [i.e. the Son of Man] stands before the Lord of spirits, and his glory is for ever and ever. . . . In him dwells the spirit of wisdom and the spirit which gives insight. . . . And he shall judge the secret things, and none shall be able to utter a lying word before him" (En. 49 : 1-4). "And in that place I saw the fountain of righteousness, which was inexhaustible. Around it were many fountains of wisdom. And all the thirsty drank of them, and were filled with wisdom, and they had their dwellings with the righteous and holy and elect" (En. 48 : 1). "The righteous shall arise from their sleep, and wisdom shall arise and be given unto them" (En. 91 : 10).

The doctrine of the participation of the Son of Man and the elect in Wisdom, regarded as a divine being, failed to make headway in eschatological thought against the older and simpler idea of participation in the Spirit of God. It is, however, possible that the notion of this dwelling of Wisdom in the Son of Man and the elect paved the way for the doctrine of the early Greek Christian theologians that the divine Logos dwelt in Jesus and was also granted to believers. There is at any rate a remarkable resemblance between the verse in the Johannine Prologue referring to the Logos, "And the light shineth in the darkness; and the darkness apprehended it not" (Jn. 1 : 5) and that in the Book of Enoch where Wisdom, when she did not find the dwelling-place she sought among the children of men, returned to her place in heaven (En. 42 : 1 f.).

The Psalms of Solomon: General

The so-called Psalms of Solomon form a short book consisting of seventeen psalm-like songs. Among them are some which would have been worthy of inclusion in the Old Testament psalter. The book was lost for a long time and was rediscovered, in a Greek translation of the original Hebrew text, only at the beginning of the seventeenth century.

Like the Book of Enoch, these psalms presuppose severe persecutions which the Pharisees are having to endure at the hands of the Hasmonean rulers and the Sadducees. In one of the psalms there is mention of the need to flee from their persecutors into the desert. "They that loved the synagogues of the pious fled from them. Like sparrows they were driven from their nest. They wandered in the desert that their lives might be saved from harm, and it seemed precious to the homeless to save their bare life from them. Over the whole earth were they scattered by the godless" (Pss. Sol. 17 : 16–18). We know for a fact from the Jewish writer Flavius Josephus (A.D. 37–95) that at one time 8,000 Pharisees had to escape to the desert.

To judge the Pharisees fairly we must take into account the sufferings they had to endure in order to preserve the religion of their fathers at the hands of the Hasmonean rulers in the first century B.C., and then again later under Herod the Great (39–4 B.C.). The spontaneous and genuine piety which finds expression in so many of the songs in the Psalms of Solomon shows them in a light different from that in which they are generally seen. "In our tribulation we call upon thee for help. And thou dost not reject our petition, for thou art our God. Cause not thy hand to be heavy upon us, lest through necessity we sin. Even though thou hearkenest to us not, we will not keep away, but will come unto thee. For if I hunger, unto thee will I cry, O God, and thou wilt give to me. . . . Who is the salvation of the poor and needy, if not thou, O Lord? And thou wilt hearken, for who is good and gentle but thou? Make glad the soul of the poor and open thine hand in mercy" (Pss. Sol. 5 : 5–12). "Turn, O God, thy mercy upon us and have pity upon us. Gather together the dispersed of Israel, with mercy and goodness, for thy faithfulness is with us. Though we have stiffened our neck, yet thou wast our chastener. Turn thyself not from us, O our God, lest the Gentiles swallow us up, as though there were none to deliver. . . . We will not depart from thee, for good are thy judgements upon us. Ours and our children's be thy good pleasure for ever. O Lord, our saviour, we would not falter any more for ever" (Pss. Sol. 8 : 27–33).

The occasion which gave rise to these psalms was the arrival of Pompeius (106–48) in Jerusalem in the year 64 to settle a dispute about the throne. Both parties invited him. Subsequently, however, in 63, he had to besiege and storm the Temple mount, which had probably been fortified to protect the Temple; our knowledge of these events comes from Josephus.[14] He penetrated into the sanctuary, and his soldiers, after a terrible blood bath, desecrated the altar of burnt offering by trampling on it.

Pompeius decided against Aristobulus II (66–33 B.C.), the persecutor of the Pharisees, and led him and his children in captivity to Rome. To the writer of the Psalms of Solomon he is the instrument of which God avails himself to punish the Hasmoneans and the Sadducees for what they have done to the pious. At the same time he sees in him the desecrator of the Temple, and in the pitiful death which he soon afterwards suffered he sees the judgement that God executes upon the transgressor. After losing the Battle of Pharsalus in 48 B.C., Pompeius had fled before Caesar to Egypt, but immediately after landing at Pelusium (near the modern Port Said), had been assassinated by order of King Ptolemy XII. His corpse remained for a long time without burial. "The heathen have reproached Jerusalem and trampled it down. . . . I saw and earnestly entreated the Lord and said, Long enough, O Lord, has thine hand been heavy on Jerusalem, in bringing the heathen upon it. . . . For not in zeal for thee have they behaved, but in the lust of their hearts, pouring out their wrath upon us in rapine. Delay not, O God, to recompense them on their heads, to turn the pride of the dragon into dishonour. And I had not long to wait before God showed me the insolent one slain on the mountains of Egypt, esteemed of less account than the least on land and sea, his body borne hither and thither on the billows with much tossing, and no one buried him because he had given him to dishonour. He reflected not that he was man, and reflected not on the latter end; He said, I will be lord of land and sea, and he recognized not that it is God who is great, mighty in his great strength. He is king in heaven and judges kings and kingdoms" (Psalms of Solomon 2 : 19–30).

---

[14] Shortly after the reconsecration of the Temple in 165 Judas Maccabeus fortified the Temple mount (1 Macc. 4 : 60 f.). In the year 142 his brother Simon extended the fortifications (1 Macc. 13 : 52 f.).

The Psalms of Solomon: The Messiah and his Kingdom

The expectation of the Kingdom that we glean from these hymns is in no way influenced by Daniel and Enoch. It keeps exclusively to Isaiah, Jeremiah, Ezekiel and Deutero-Isaiah. What is hoped for is the coming of the Davidic Messiah. There is no mention of the Son of Man. The songs express joy that God has brought to an end the reign of the Hasmoneans, who had set themselves upon the throne of David. They had thought to make an end of God's promise to David that his kingdom should endure for ever. Now it is plain that they were wrong. One day God will cause the Messiah of David's line to appear. "For our sins godless men rose up against us. . . . With pomp they crowned themselves in their pride, they laid waste the throne of David in tumultuous arrogance. But thou, O God, didst cast them down and remove their seed from the earth, in that there rose up against them a man that was alien to our race" (Pss. Sol. 17 : 5–7). "Behold, O Lord, and raise up unto them their king, the son of David, in the time when thou choosest, O God, that he should reign over thy servant Israel. And gird him with strength, that he may shatter unrighteous rulers, and that he may purge Jerusalem from the heathen that trample her down to destruction. . . . Then he will gather together a holy people, whom he shall rule in righteousness, and he shall judge the tribes of the people that has been sanctified by the Lord his God" (Pss. Sol. 17 : 21 f., 26).

Through his study of the scriptures the writer has identified himself with the hopes for the future of the ancient prophets. We find in him a revival of the conception of the Messianic Kingdom which presupposes the existence of the kingship of the House of David, or at least (in the Exile and in Haggai and Zechariah) an expectation of its re-establishment. But does the writer really assume that it will be re-established like this after all these centuries? Or does he think of the Davidic Messiah as a supernatural being who will come from heaven? The latter view must be the correct one.

The writer of the songs presupposes that the resurrection has taken place. But if human beings participate in the Kingdom in their resurrection form, it must be a supernatural entity. The Messianic king of the early prophets can no longer be thought of as its ruler. "The destruction of the sinner is for ever, and he shall not be remembered, when the righteous is visited. This is the portion of sinners for ever. But they that fear the Lord shall rise to life eternal, and their life shall be in the light of the Lord and shall come to an end no more" (Pss. Sol. 3 : 11 f.).

The only question is whether the writer of the songs is clear in his mind that the participation of those who have risen from the dead makes the Kingdom of God something different from what it was for the prophets of old, and that this necessitates a different conception of the Messiah. We have to reckon with the possibility that he clung to the old view though it was no longer tenable. There are, in fact, many indications that he has not entirely harmonized expectation of the future with belief in the resurrection. For instance, he does not mention that those who are still alive at the coming of the Kingdom will undergo a transformation when they enter it to adapt them to a supernatural form of existence like those who have risen. The question whether aliens and sojourners can live in it (Pss. Sol. 17 : 28) does not fit in with the picture of a Kingdom which is the home of those who have risen, nor does the idea that the heathen nations will serve under the Messiah's yoke and nations come from the end of the earth to Jerusalem to see his glory (Pss. Sol. 17 : 30 f.). These aliens, sojourners and heathen are, of course, still in their natural state.

The Psalms of Solomon do not assume a resurrection of all the dead to judgement. Only the righteous awake to their new existence. It is by the resurrection that they are marked as belonging to the Kingdom. The dead who do not take part in the resurrection are thereby shown to be sinners. They will share the fate of those who on the Day of Judgement are still alive and are sentenced to "perish for ever" (Pss. Sol. 15 : 13). The Messiah allows only those whom he acknowledges as "sons of God" to dwell in the Kingdom (Pss. Sol. 17 : 27).

The theory, going back to Ezekiel, that in the final tribulation those who are to enter the Kingdom remain alive under God's protection is the only common ground which the Psalms of Solomon have with the Book of Enoch. "For the mark of God is upon the righteous that they may be saved. Famine and sword and pestilence shall be far from the righteous; they shall flee away from the pious as men pursued in battle; but they shall pursue the ungodly and overtake them. . . . As by enemies experienced in war shall they be overtaken, for the mark of destruction is upon their forehead" (Pss. Sol. 15 : 6–9).

The Apocalypses of Baruch and Ezra. Problems of Belief

The two last apocalypses of late Judaism presuppose the destruction of Jerusalem by Titus in A.D. 70, and refer to it. One of them purports to come from Baruch, the friend of Jeremiah to whom he dictated his prophecies (Jer. 36 : 4), the other from Ezra, the priest and scribe who in 458 led a second caravan out of captivity to Jerusalem. The Apocalypse of Ezra is generally referred to as the Fourth Book of Ezra (4 Ezra). The explanation of this is that in the Vulgate (the Latin translation of the Bible revised by the learned church father Jerome, who lived from 345 to 420, and later given official recognition) the two books which are found in the Old Testament as Ezra and Nehemiah count as the First and Second Books of Ezra. There was added a Third Book (3 Ezra), an unimportant writing ascribed to Ezra, but probably dating from the end of the first century B.C.; it contains excerpts from Ezra, Nehemiah and 1 and 2 Chronicles. The Apocalypse of Ezra was therefore reckoned as the Fouth Book of Ezra. The Apocalypse of Baruch is preserved in a Syriac translation, that of Ezra in Latin, Syriac, Ethiopic, Arabic and Armenian.

Through its presence in many MSS. of the Vulgate, the apocalypse of Ezra, undoubtedly the most important work of late Judaism, remained known to the Christianity of the West. Luther disliked it. The visions that appear in it did not appeal to him, and he would have liked to throw the visionary who wrote it into the Elbe.

The writers of the Apocalypses of Baruch and Ezra look forward from the age in which they are supposed to have lived and survey the course of history from the first destruction of Jerusalem by the Babylonians in 586 to the second, by Titus, which they have actually experienced. This catastrophe is the basis of their writing. The Baruch work seems to be somewhat older than that of Ezra, which was completed in its present form before the death of Domitian in A.D. 96. The main body of the text, however, probably belongs to a time closer to the year 70.

Both books are similar in form and content. They consist of visions, in which the writers discuss with angels and with God the religious problems that occupy their mind. The most prominent are the incomprehensible way in which God again and again delivers his people into the hands of the Gentiles and twice allows Jerusalem to be destroyed; the universal sinfulness which goes back to Adam and neutralizes the remedial effect that the Law ought to have; the delay in the coming of the Kingdom; and the destiny allotted to sinners who repent only at the last Judgement. The range of problems is wider in Ezra than in Baruch, and he goes more deeply into them. In many respects Baruch looks like a preliminary draft of Ezra.

In answer to their complaint that God has twice allowed Jerusalem to be destroyed, Baruch and Ezra are told that the Jerusalem that was rebuilt after the return from the Exile still belongs to the temporal world. The prophecies concerning Jerusalem, on the other hand, refer to the heavenly city, created by God at the beginning of the world and shown to Adam (before the Fall) and Abraham. Both find it incomprehensible that the Gentiles, who completely disregard God's Law, come off better than the people of God, who have striven to live by it, and to whom the promises apply.

An entirely new development in the religious thought of Judaism is the way in which Baruch and Ezra derive the sinfulness of man and all the misery that has resulted from it from Adam's sin in Paradise. "O Adam, what hast thou done to all those who are born from thee! And what will be said to the first Eve who hearkened to the serpent? For all this multitude are going to corruption, nor is there any numbering of those whom the fire devours" (Bar. 48 : 42 f.). "O Adam, what hast thou done? For though it was thou who didst sin, the fall was not thine alone, but ours also who are thy descendants! For how does it profit us that the eternal age is promisĕd to us, whereas we have done the works that bring death? (4 Ez. 7 : 118 f.).

When God revealed the Law to his people after the Exodus from Egypt, he promised them that through it they would inherit eternal glory. Now, however, it has come about that "we who have received the Law must perish for our sins, along with our heart, which has taken it in: the Law, however, perishes not, but abides in its glory" (4 Ez. 9 : 36 f.). Baruch and Ezra cannot come to terms with the fact that, through Adam's sin, practically all men are to perish, and only the small number of those who have summoned up the strength to become righteous in spite of their inherited sinfulness can be saved. Why, asks Ezra, has God, when it lay in his power, not prevented men from doing evil? Why has he not chastised his people with his own hand when they sinned, so as to recall them to the right path, instead of handing them over to the Gentiles for punishment? Again and again it comes back to this, that it would have been better if men had never appeared upon earth at all than that they should be sentenced for their sin to the kind of existence in which they now live. To comfort him, God allows him to see in a vision the heavenly Jerusalem (4 Ez. 9 : 38–10 : 58), and to know that he himself has no need to fear the judgement, since he has a "treasure of good works laid up with the Most High" (4 Ez. 7 : 77). Indeed, he will not die at all, but be taken up to heaven, to live with the Messiah until the times are ended (4 Ez. 14 : 9). But Ezra will not be put off from his concern with the fate of all men. He wrestles with the angel and with God in moving passages. He will not be pacified with the reply, "This world the Most High has created for many, but that which is to come for few" (4 Ez. 8 : 1), or, "Many have been created, but few shall be saved" (4 Ez. 8 : 3), or with the advice, "Do thou rather think of thine own case and search out the glory which thy brothers shall inherit" (4 Ez. 8 : 51). God reproves him with the words, "Thou comest far short of being able to love my creation more than I" (4 Ez. 8 : 47), but his heart will not let him remain silent.

To the question whether sinners can still obtain salvation
through repentance on the Day of Judgement, Baruch and Ezra
receive the answer that repentance is possible only in the present
age, and not hereafter in the Day of Judgement, which belongs to
the end of time (Baruch 85 : 12; 4 Ez. 9 : 10–12). This answer is in
contradiction to that received by Enoch (En. 50 : 1–3), according
to which God in his compassion will forgive sinners if they make
repentance "on the day of affliction, on which evil has been
treasured up against them", and they then become witnesses of
the good fortune which comes to the righteous.[15]

There remains one last hope to Ezra: perhaps the righteous
can intercede for sinners with God by their petitions. To his
question whether this is possible he receives the same answer as
Baruch (Bar. 85 : 12–15), that this cannot be. On the Day of
Judgement "None shall pray for another, nor shall anyone accuse
another; for then every one shall bear his own righteousness or
unrighteousness" (4 Ez. 7 : 102–105). Ezra cites the precedent that
Abraham prayed for the people of Sodom, Moses for the people
of Israel, as did Joshua and others after him. If righteous men
could then make petition for sinners, why should this not be done
at the Judgement? The angel informs him that this can happen
in the present world, which is passing away, but is no longer
possible on the Day of Judgement, which means the end of this
world (4 Ez. 7 : 106–115). Thereupon Ezra begins to make petition
to God while there is still time: "O Lord, who dwellest in heaven,
. . . hear thy servant's prayer. . . . For so long as I live I must
speak, and while I possess understanding answer. Look not on the
sins of thy people, but on them that have served thee in truth.
Regard not the deeds of the transgressors, but rather them that
have kept thy covenants in the midst of sufferings. Think not
upon those who have walked deceitfully before thee, but hold
in remembrance those who have laboured in thy service with all
their heart. . . . For the righteous, who have many works laid
up with thee, shall out of their own deeds receive their reward.
But what is man, that thou shouldst be wroth with him? Or
what is a corruptible race, that thou canst be so bitter towards it?

[15] See p. 48.

For in truth there is none born of woman who has not sinned, not one of those who live who has not come short. For in this, O Lord, shall thy righteousness and goodness be manifest, that thou hast compassion for them that have no treasure of good works" (4 Ez. 8 : 20–36).

Baruch and Ezra: The Kingdom of the Messiah and the Kingdom of God

With regard to their eschatological expectation, Baruch and Ezra set themselves the task of achieving an organic integration of the expectation of the resurrection of the dead and that of the Kingdom. The writer of the Psalms of Solomon has not yet grasped the problem of bringing the new idea into harmony with the old. He accepts the resurrection of the dead, but continues to hold the view of the earlier prophets about the Kingdom of the Davidic Messiah, which had no such thing in view. Daniel and the writer of Enoch solve the problem by simply giving up the old where it is incompatible with the new. They replace the Kingdom of the Davidic Messiah with that of the Son of Man, which only appears after the general resurrection of the dead and includes the survivors of the final generation, transformed into angelic beings, and the righteous of all previous generations, who are in a similar state after rising from the dead.

This solution could not be accepted by scribes well versed in the scriptures. It was impossible for them to abandon altogether the notion of the Kingdom of the Davidic Messiah which had been set down in the writings of Isaiah, Jeremiah, Ezekiel and Deutero-Isaiah. On the other hand, they found in Amos and Hosea, in portions of the Book of Isaiah (Is. 24–27 et al.), in Deutero-Zechariah (Zech. 9–14), in Malachi and in Joel, a Kingdom in which it is not the Messiah but God himself who judges and reigns. Thus two different Kingdoms had been foretold, that of the Davidic Messiah and that of God. This provided them with a solution of the problem that had arisen through the emergence of belief in the resurrection. They suppose that participation in the Kingdom of the Messiah is the privilege of the survivors of the final generation, and this is indeed the view of Isaiah, Jeremiah, Ezekiel, Deutero-Isaiah, Haggai and the authentic part of the Book of Zechariah (Zech. 1-8).

This Kingdom, in which the participants, without having been transformed into supernatural beings, lead a blessed existence in a transfigured world, is not regarded by the Apocalypses of Baruch and Ezra as everlasting. In their view it will be followed by the general resurrection, the Judgement which is to be conducted by God, and the completely supernatural Kingdom of God. This second, eternal Kingdom will be shared by the righteous of all generations, who will have become supernatural, angel-like beings through the resurrection, together with those righteous survivors of the final generation who had previously belonged to the Kingdom of the Messiah. At the appearance of the Kingdom of God they will be transformed into the same supernatural form as those who have risen from the dead.

This clever solution of the problem can reasonably claim to be scriptural. It goes beyond scripture only in one or two necessary corollaries. The Messiah is not an earth-born king raised to Messiahship, but a being who comes from heaven to earth. The two kingdoms follow one another in succession, and consequently, contrary to the view of the earlier prophets, the Messianic Kingdom does not last for ever but is only the prelude to the everlasting Kingdom of God.

The transition of the Messianic Kingdom into the Kingdom of God does not take the same course in Ezra as in Baruch. The latter says nothing about its duration and makes the Messiah return to heaven when it comes to an end (Bar. 30 : 1), whereupon the resurrection of the dead ensues. In Ezra the Messianic Kingdom lasts for 400 years. When this time is completed, the Messiah dies, together with all in whom there is human breath. The resurrection of the dead follows seven days later (4 Ez. 7 : 28-32).

Baruch and Ezra: The Events of the Final Age

The course of events in the final age is essentially the same in Baruch and Ezra. As regards its date, they are both informed by

the angels who instruct them that the world's youth is past
(Bar. 85 : 10); in fact, it has already grown old (4 Ez. 5 : 55) and
redemption is not so far distant as aforetime (Bar. 23 : 7). The
number both of those who are to be born and of the dead whom
the underworld is to receive is almost fulfilled (Bar. 23 : 3–5).
When it is fulfilled, nothing, "not even the sins of those who
dwell on earth", can stop the final events from taking place. The
dwelling of souls in Hades is like the mother's womb: as this
cannot keep back the birth when the time has come, so Hades
cannot keep the souls of the dead any longer than is appointed
(4 Ez. 4 : 38–42).

According to Ezra the history of the world falls into twelve
periods of equal length. At the time when he claims to be engaged in writing his book (thirty years after the destruction of
Jerusalem by the Babylonians in 586 B.C.), nine and a half have
passed (4 Ez. 14 : 11 f.). The fourth empire, which appears to
him in a vision of an eagle rising out of the sea, is, according to
the instruction he receives from an angel, not the Greek Empire
of Alexander the Great ("as it once appeared to thy brother
Daniel, but was not interpreted to him as I shall now interpret
it to thee"), but the Roman Empire. From the details of the vision
it becomes clear that the Roman emperors down to the time of
Domitian (81–96) are known to the writer (4 Ez. 12 : 10–30).

The righteous who are destined to die in this age (before the
events of the final age) can leave this life full of joyful confidence.
They know that they have "a treasure of good works laid up in
the store-chambers", ensuring that "they will receive the world
which they have been promised" (Bar. 14 : 11–13). They are not
afraid of the sufferings they have to endure, for they will have
their reward. "Rejoice in the sufferings which you are suffering
now", Baruch says to them by way of comfort (Bar. 52 : 5–7). As
the world grows older, the sufferings that fall upon its inhabitants
multiply. For "the truth must withdraw further off and the lie
come nearer at hand" (4 Ez. 14 : 15–17).

The arrival of the final age will be indicated by wonderful
events in nature and the occurrence of the pre-Messianic tribulation. All the righteous in Israel who are still alive will be pre-

served during this under God's protection, so that they may participate in the Messianic Kingdom. "When the time of the world is ripe and the harvest of the evil and the good has come, the Almighty will bring upon the earth and its inhabitants and upon its rulers confusion of spirit and paralysing terror. And they shall hate one another and provoke one another to war. . . . And every man who is saved from the war shall die through an earthquake, and he who escapes from the earthquake shall be burned in the fire, and all who escape and survive all these perils will be delivered into the hands of my servant, the Messiah. For the whole earth shall devour its inhabitants. But the holy land will have mercy on him who belongs to it and will protect its inhabitants in that time" (Bar. 70 : 1-3, 8-71 : 1).

The appearance of the Messiah brings an end to the tribulation. "Then will the Messiah begin to be revealed. . . . The earth shall yield its fruit ten thousandfold. On each vine there will be a thousand shoots, and each shoot will bear a thousand clusters and a cluster will have a thousand grapes. . . . And at that time the treasury of manna shall again descend from on high. And they will eat of it in those years because they have lived to the end of the times" (Bar. 29 : 3-8). "Then shall healing descend in dew and disease shall be taken away. . . . And no one shall die before his time nor shall any adversity suddenly befall. . . . And the wild beasts shall come from the forest and minister to men. . . . And then shall women no longer have pain when they give birth" (Bar. 73 : 2-7).

In the Messianic Kingdom, as Baruch and Ezra conceive it, in common with the Psalms of Solomon and the early prophets, men live in a transfigured, but not yet completely supernatural, world. In a beautiful passage in Baruch, it belongs to the time when "it is the end of that which is corruptible and the beginning of that which is incorruptible" (Bar. 74 : 2).

In the Messianic Kingdom the heavenly Jerusalem, come down to earth, and Paradise both have their place (4 Ez. 7 : 26). Only those who survive from the final generation, not those who rise from the dead, belong to it. Baruch and Ezra cannot permit themselves to go into the difficulties connected with the concep-

tion of the Messiah "whom the most High has kept for the end
of days, who shall spring from the seed of David and shall appear"
(4 Ez. 12 : 32). They are compelled to ignore them, because they
have no solution to them. They cannot but assume that he comes
from heaven, since rulers of David's line are no longer to be
found on earth. It is therefore inconceivable that God should
bestow his Spirit upon an earthly ruler and thereby make him
Messiah. On the other hand, they cannot simply give up the
view of the prophets (written at a time when there still were
kings of David's line) that the Messiah stems from David, since
it is written in the scriptures. Accordingly they have to claim
that he is descended from David, and at the same time is a being
who comes from heaven.

The only possible solution of the problem would be to assume
that the Messiah is a descendant of David born in the final
generation, who begins his reign only after he has become a
supernatural being as a result of having risen from the dead. This
is the only way in which it would be possible for a Messiah
thought of as a supernatural being to be in fact a descendant of
David. This is the solution underlying the Messianic self-
consciousness of Jesus.

According to Baruch and Ezra the Messiah will reprove the
last ruler of the Roman Empire for his ungodliness and destroy
him (Bar. 40 : 1 f.; 4 Ez. 12 : 32 f.). Of all the nations still in
existence, he will spare only those which have not been enemies
of Israel (Bar. 72 : 2–6). In Baruch and Ezra, as in the Psalms of
Solomon, he does not execute judgement on the survivors of the
people of Israel. They are revealed as having their place in the
Messianic Kingdom since they were preserved in the tribulation.
In Baruch the Messianic Kingdom is then transformed into the
everlasting Kingdom of God. He thus assumes that those who
participate in the Messianic Kingdom are subsequently transformed
into angel-like beings, and that those who have risen from the
dead and survived God's judgement will attain to the same state
and be added to their number.

It is interesting to note that in his view these rise from the dead
with the same body and form that they had before they died,

and only later obtain their supernatural form. "And it shall come to pass after these things, when the time of the advent of the Messiah is fulfilled, that he shall return to heaven in glory. Then all who have fallen asleep in hope of him shall rise again. And it shall come to pass at that time that the treasure chambers will be opened in which is preserved the number of the souls of the righteous, and they shall come forth, and a multitude of souls shall be seen together in one assemblage of one thought, and the first shall rejoice and the last shall not be grieved. For each one knows that the time has come of which it is said that it is the end of the times. But the souls of the ungodly, when they behold all these things, shall then pine away from fear. For they know that their torment has come and their downfall has arrived" (Bar. 30 : 1–5). "For the righteous, however, there shall then be glory surpassing that of the angels. . . . For they were delivered from this world of tribulation and put from them the burden of their anguish" (Bar. 51 : 12–14).

Ezra makes the Messiah die, along with those who shared in his Kingdom. In his view, therefore, all who belong to the human race, even the Messiah of David's line, who was already with God in heaven, must pass through death and resurrection before they can become angelic beings. "And it shall be, after these [400] years, that my son, the Messiah, shall die, and all in whom there is human breath. Then shall the world be turned into the primeval silence seven days, as at the first beginning; so that no man is left. But after seven days shall the aeon which is still asleep awake and that which is corruptible shall perish. The earth shall restore those that are at rest in her and the dust those that sleep therein. The chambers shall restore those that were committed to them. The most High shall appear upon the throne of judgement" (4 Ez. 7 : 29–33).

Ezra raises the question whether those who die before the time of tribulation and so avoid suffering it, or those who experience its terrors and survive, should be considered the more fortunate. He receives from God the answer, "Know, therefore, that those who survive it are more blessed than those who have died" (4 Ez. 13 : 24). This reply to Ezra conflicts with the revelation given to Enoch. The latter read "on the heavenly tablets" that the lot of those who have died is better than that of the living (En. 103 : 3). The difference in the answers goes back to a difference in their views of the Kingdom. Enoch looks forward to a single Kingdom. For him the dead have the advantage over the living because they attain the same blessedness without having to undergo the pre-Messianic tribulation. In Ezra there are two Kingdoms to be taken into account, the Messianic and, after that, the everlasting Kingdom of God. The dead participate only in the latter, the living in both. The disadvantage of suffering the pre-Messianic tribulation is more than outweighed by the subsequent twofold blessedness. That is why in Ezra "those who survive are more blessed than those who have died". Ezra attaches great importance to establishing that, as the world was created by God and him alone, he alone will "make visitation upon his creation", and its end will come through him "and none else" (4 Ez. 6 : 1–6). This can only mean that he regards it as necessary to refute the opinion that God does not conduct the judgement himself and does not himself reign in the everlasting Kingdom, a view represented by Daniel and Enoch. According to the former God delegates the governing of his Kingdom to the Son of Man, and according to the latter the previous conduct of the judgement as well. Ezra attacks them without mentioning them by name. In his eschatology, as in Baruch's, there is no place for the Son of Man.

This seems to be contradicted by the fact that in the section 4 Ezra 13 : 1–18, 25–27 we are told of the Son of Man that he comes on the clouds of heaven, destroys a great host with the fiery breath of his mouth as he comes from Mount Zion, and is then surrounded by the multitude of the ten tribes of Israel returning from captivity. This section, however, does not come from the writer of the apocalypse, but has been added at the end by a later writer. He sees that the Son of Man is missing in Ezra and seeks to repair the omission by giving him a part to play. He has, however, no real conception of his personality. Not noticing that he belongs to the time after the resurrection, he makes him, like the Messiah, appear in the time that precedes it.

All he does is to make him an unimportant double of the Messiah. This Son of Man section is in every way in contrast with the main text. It conflicts with the plan of the whole work. The section (4 Ezra 13 : 13–24) dealing with the question whether the lot of those who have died or of those who survive is the better forms a kind of erratic block between the vision of the Son of Man and its interpretation. This shows that there has been interference with the text of the concluding section.

The Meaning of the World of Thought of Baruch and Ezra

Through the Apocalypses of Baruch and Ezra we obtain an insight into the piety of the scribes of the first century A.D. which we should never have known or suspected had they not been preserved. This piety was concerned with problems whose existence we should not have expected in late Judaism. They are problems which occupied the attention of the Apostle Paul, as we know from his letters written between A.D. 50 and 62. It was not, therefore, only after his conversion that they occurred to him; they were in his mind when he was still a scribe living among scribes. He finds the solution to them in his faith that Jesus was the Messiah and that in consequence of his death the Messianic Kingdom was about to arrive. His view of the final events likewise comes from that of the scribes, as preserved for us in the Apocalypses of Baruch and Ezra. Like them, he expects, according to 1 Cor. 15 : 23–28, two Kingdoms: first the Messianic, in which Jesus reigns, and after that the everlasting Kingdom of God. Like them, he does not speak of the Son of Man, though Jesus had used this expression of himself. Like them, he is concerned to establish that in the everlasting Kingdom which follows the resurrection of the dead no one but God comes into consideration (1 Cor. 15 : 28).

It may well be assumed that Baruch and Ezra have taken account of Christianity and rejected its eschatology, like that of Daniel and Enoch, without mentioning it by name. At the time they were writing Christianity had been in existence for at least four decades. They certainly knew of it. Why do they not attack its view that the Messiah had previously existed as a man living in this world? The reason why these two writings ignore Christianity in this way is probably that their object is to bring to a final conclusion the undertaking in which the scribes had been engaged for a considerable time, long before the appearance of Jesus. This was to reduce to order the various traditional views of the Messianic Kingdom and the Kingdom of God. They are dealing only with material from the past, not with innovations.

The fact that there is no mention of Jesus or Christianity in the two important Jewish works that deal with the question of the Messiah and the Kingdom of God after the year 70 provides the strongest argument that those who dispute the historical existence of Jesus could possibly adduce. They have never as yet made use of it.

CHAPTER II

THE KINGDOM OF GOD IN THE TEACHING OF JESUS

I. JOHN THE BAPTIST AND JESUS

The Gospels of Matthew and Mark as Sources

Historical research into the beginnings of Christianity began in the last quarter of the eighteenth century. Its subject matter was the public appearance and preaching of John the Baptist and Jesus of Nazareth. At first it was hoped that the reports of the four evangelists could be brought into harmony with one another. From the middle of the nineteenth century, however, it was recognized by scholarship based on scientific historical method that this was impossible, and that the only Gospels which agree with one another and therefore come into consideration are those of Matthew and Mark. The Gospel of Luke offers a later understanding of the traditions represented by the first two. The Fourth is completely incompatible with them. It makes Jerusalem the main scene of Jesus' activity, whereas according to Matthew and Mark he goes there with his disciples only once, for the Passover, and that is in order to die there. The Fourth Gospel also attributes to him a type of preaching quite different from that found in Matthew and Mark.

Ferdinand Christian Baur (1792–1860), the great Tübingen scholar, and his school regarded Matthew as the oldest and original Gospel. From the middle of the nineteenth century, as a result of Hermann Weisse's *Die Evangelienfrage* (1856) and Heinrich Julius Holtzmann's *Die synoptischen Evangelien* (1863), priority was accorded to Mark.

The question which of the two Gospels gives us the account closest to the original cannot be answered. Neither of them has come down to us in its original form. In both, for instance, an apocalypse of the early Christian period, purporting to be a sermon of Jesus and dealing with the delay in the coming of the

Kingdom and the Son of Man, has been interpolated into the text (Mk. 13 : 1–37; Mt. 24 : 1–51). So far as the addition in this way of later pieces of material is concerned, Mark's Gospel has the advantage over Matthew's. It begins with an account of the appearance of the Baptist and ends with the description of how Mary Magdalene, Mary the daughter of James, and Salome came to the tomb early on the morning after the Sabbath with spices to anoint the body of Jesus, found the tomb empty, were told by a young man in white clothing that he had risen, and received from him the commission to inform the disciples (Mk. 16 : 1–8).[1]

The account in Matthew adds to this that Jesus appeared to the women and later showed himself to the disciples in Galilee, where he commanded them to preach the gospel in the whole world and to baptize believers in the name of the Father, the Son and the Holy Spirit. This concluding section must have been added comparatively late, since it was only after a lapse of time that the names of Father, Son and Spirit came into use.

The beginning of Matthew was enriched later with the genealogy of Jesus, designed to prove his descent from David, and the stories of his birth, the coming of the wise men from the East, and the flight into Egypt (Mt. 1 and 2). The advantage that Matthew has over Mark is that, in addition to the source which it has in common with Mark, it has made use of another. This too includes stories and speeches which obviously belong to the earliest tradition. We owe to it our knowledge of the Sermon on the Mount and the Lord's Prayer (Mt. 5–7), the great sermon at the sending out of the disciples (Mt. 10), the Baptist's question to Jesus whether he is "he that should come" and his reply with the appended speech to the people about the Baptist (Mt. 11), the great denunciation of the Pharisees (Mt. 23), the Parable of the Talents and the subsequent sermon on the judgement which the Son of Man will conduct (Mt. 25), with which Jesus concludes his preaching in the Temple.

Those who sought to give the primacy to Mark were led to

---

[1] In later MSS. an ending has been added to Mark in which there is a description of appearances of the risen Lord, and a reunion with the disciples in which he speaks of baptism and his ascension (Mk. 16 : 9–20).

this conclusion by its brevity and the prospect it opened of enabling them to find in this Gospel the outline of the course of Jesus' public ministry. They thought that they might take it from Mark that a period of successful activity was followed by one of growing opposition, in the course of which the people fell away from him more and more, so that he came to the conclusion that he must die for the cause of the Kingdom of God. In the eyes of those who see in Mark's Gospel the real source of our knowledge of Jesus, it has the further advantage that, because of its brevity, the agreement of Jesus' expectation of the Kingdom of God with late Jewish eschatology is far less noticeable than in Matthew, which is twice as long.

This interpretation of the Marcan narrative is inadmissible. Historical research has to consider not only which account may be the older, but also which is the fuller. We cannot tell from Mark alone, but only from him and Matthew together, which occurrences in the course of his ministry were important to Jesus and drove him to the conclusion that it was God's destiny for him that he should die. For this some of the passages found only in Matthew are of the highest importance.

How does it stand with the accounts which Mark and Matthew have in common? Which of them gives the original text here? In a number of passages it seems to be the shorter text of Mark. This is also the impression he makes in some of the details he reports. On the whole, however, the theory that his shorter text should be preferred to Matthew's longer cannot be sustained. There are places where it is difficult to avoid the conclusion that his text is the result of omissions. He gives us, for instance, only a few sentences from the sermon of Jesus at the sending out of the disciples, which in Matthew is a firmly constructed whole. The meaning of their mission, that they are to hasten through the cities of Israel with the message that the coming of God's Kingdom is now close at hand, is not at all clear. The saying of Jesus that the manifestation of the Son of Man will take place before they have completed their journey through the cities of Israel is missing altogether (Mk. 6 : 7–13).

Mark's account of the incident at Caesarea Philippi also depends on an abbreviation of the text of the common source. After Peter has replied, to the question of Jesus about whom the disciples think him to be, that he is the Messiah, in Matthew Jesus pronounces him blessed, in that God has revealed to him what he could not have learned from any man, and because of this accords him a special position. He then forbids the disciples to divulge to anyone that he is the Messiah (Mt. 16 : 13–20). In Mark he does not give Peter, who is in possession of this knowledge, a word of acknowledgement, but comes out immediately with the prohibition which in Matthew comes later, and then, like him, goes on to proclaim that he must suffer and die (Mk. 8 : 29–33).

The position, then, is that when they vary from one another in their report of common material, sometimes Mark and sometimes Matthew gives the impression of giving us the original text, and a clear decision is not possible in every instance. We are dealing with an insoluble literary problem. The sources used by Mark and Matthew in common, as well as the special material of Matthew, go back to men who were present during the ministry of Jesus. They have in the main a clear conception of the order of events and give a reliable report of the speeches of Jesus. They do not attribute to him any views different from those of the late Jewish expectation of the Kingdom and the Messiah. This shows that their account is basically historical.

The trustworthiness of the two oldest Gospels is further demonstrated by the fact that they record words and acts of Jesus which of necessity remained incomprehensible to those who heard and saw them, and also by the fact that they quote prophecies which were not fulfilled. It is therefore untrue that we know nothing certain about Jesus. The two oldest Gospels give us a reliable and detailed account of his preaching and his public ministry, which extended over only a few months. They are a priceless treasure which has not been properly appreciated. It is little short of a miracle that so true a record of Jesus has been preserved.

The two oldest Gospels probably became known in their original form in Palestine about A.D. 70. The Gospel of Luke appeared after the first two, but probably before the end of the

first century. It comes from the same author as the Acts of the
Apostles and presupposes the existence of earlier written Gospels
(Lk. 1 : 1–4). The Fourth Gospel probably appeared at the
beginning of the second century. It presupposes Christians from
the Hellenistic world and the doctrine of the Logos as a mode of
divine manifestation. Because it comes so long after the others
and makes Jesus preach a different message from the other three,
it had difficulty in winning acceptance alongside of them in the
canon of New Testament scriptures.

The Date of the Appearance of the Baptist and Jesus

When did the Baptist and Jesus make their appearance? We can
calculate only the approximate year of Jesus' death. Since he was
crucified under Pontius Pilate, this must have occurred before
36. Pilate was governor of Judaea, Samaria and Idumaea from
26 to 36. We have a further piece of evidence for the approximate
calculation of the year of Jesus' death in an inscription discovered
at Delphi in 1905. We can conclude from this that Gallio, the
brother of the Roman philosopher Seneca (A.D. 2–66), occupied
the office of proconsul of Achaea from May 51 to May 52.
According to Acts, Paul was haled before the bench of this Gallio
by the Jews while he was staying in Corinth during the Second
Missionary Journey (Acts 18 : 12–16). We know from remarks
of Paul in the Epistle to the Galatians (Gal. 1 : 17–2 : 2) that
seventeen years passed between his conversion and his meeting
with the Apostles in Jerusalem (Gal. 2 : 1–10 and Acts 15 : 1–35),
at which the questions relating to Gentile Christians were
discussed. The Second Missionary Journey, which took Paul
to Corinth by way of Antioch, Lystra, Troas, Philippi, Thessalo-
nica and Athens, took place after this meeting. We may reckon
at least two years for the journey from Jerusalem, with a stay
in several cities. We may also assume, as is clear from Acts
18 : 12, 18, that Paul was brought before Gallio soon after his
arrival in Corinth, i.e. in the year 51, and that his conversion took
place from one to two years after the death of Jesus. We must

therefore subtract from 51 2 (or 1)+17+1 (or 2), that is to say about twenty or twenty-one years, to reach the approximate date of the death of Jesus. It would then fall in about the year 30.

As we need, according to the two earliest Gospels, to allow hardly a year for the public ministry of Jesus, and the prior activity of the Baptist was of no long duration, the latter will have taken place round about the year 28. The statement of Luke (Lk. 3 : 1 f.) that the Baptist appeared in the fifteenth year of the Emperor Tiberius (14–37), i.e. between the autumn of 28 and that of 29, is in agreement with this. According to Luke (Lk. 3 : 23), Jesus at his appearance was "about thirty years old".

The pagan historians of the earliest period after Jesus derive their knowledge of him from the popular opinion of Christianity and its founder. The first to mention Christianity and Jesus is Tacitus (56–118) in the Annals (XV, 44), written under Trajan in the second decade of the second century. He records that Nero, in order to silence the rumour that he had set Rome on fire, put forward as the persons responsible some people detested for their crimes, whom the people called Christians, on whom he then inflicted the most elaborate punishments. The originator of this name, Christ, he goes on to say, was executed by the procurator Pontius Pilate in the reign of Tiberius. Later, however, this detestable superstition, which had been suppressed for the moment, broke out again, not only in Judaea, where it originated, but also in the city of Rome, where everything shameful from the whole world tends to make its way and find support.[2]

Suetonius (69–141), in the 25th chapter of his biography of the Emperor Claudius, reveals an even scantier knowledge of Jesus and Christianity. He reports of the violent tumults which took place among the Jewish population of Rome about the year 50 that a certain Chrestus was their instigator. These tumults can

[2] Ergo abolendo rumori Nero subdidit reos et quaesitissimis poenis adfecit, quos per flagitia invisos vulgus Christianos appellabat. Autor nominis eius Christus Tiberio imperitante per procuratorem Pontium Pilatum supplicio adfectus erat, repressaque in praesens exitiabilis superstitio rursum erumpebat, nonmodo per Judaeam originem eius mali, sed per urbem etiam quo cuncta undique atrocia aut pudenda confluunt celebranturque (Tac., *Ann.* XV, 44).

only refer to the Jewish opposition to the Christians. As a result of these occurrences the Jews were expelled from Rome.[3]

Among the Jewish Christians expelled along with the Jews from Rome at this time were Aquila and his wife Priscilla, with whom Paul lived and worked in Corinth between 51 and 52, since they, like him, followed the craft of tent-making (i.e. the weaving of canvas) (Acts 18 : 2 f.).

John the Baptist: The Novelty of his Preaching

About the year 28, at the time when Pontius Pilate was governor of Judaea under the Emperor Tiberius and Herod Antipas was ruling Galilee as king, the hermit John came forward with a message of the Kingdom of God that was something completely new. For centuries the Kingdom of God had been mentioned only in writings claiming to have been written by holy men in the remote past. Now a prophet had once more appeared, speaking about the Kingdom of God to his contemporaries. Another novelty was the fact that he was not driven to speak about its coming by reason of some historical event that had just occurred. He was not even, like the writers of the apocalypses, calculating the conditions which would have to be fulfilled before it could arrive. He simply preaches that the time has come. "And in those days cometh John the Baptist, preaching in the wilderness of Judaea, saying, Repent ye; for the Kingdom of heaven is at hand" (Mt. 3 : 1 f.).

John does not concern himself with a description of the final events. He is the traveller who has come to the foot of the mountains. He no longer glimpses the relative positions of the various peaks. All he cares about is being equipped to make the ascent. That is why he demands of his hearers that they repent. When the Greek word *metanoeite* ($\mu\varepsilon\tau\alpha\nu o\varepsilon\tilde{\iota}\tau\varepsilon$, change your thoughts) yields its true meaning, it is a call not only for repentance over past sins, but above all for a new way of thinking in the period of waiting for the Kingdom.

[3] Judaeos impulsore Chresto assidue tumultuantes Roma expulit (Suet., *Vita Claud.*, cap. 25).

The Baptism of John

Still more novelty! John declares that the required repentance becomes valid and effective through an act which he performs, namely baptism. All earlier prophets came forward as preachers alone. He exercises authority at the same time. His baptism is not only an act symbolizing cleansing from guilt; it actually confers salvation. To the Pharisees and Sadducees who come to be baptized by him he says: "Ye offspring of vipers, who warned you to flee from the wrath to come?" (Mt. 3 : 7). He cannot refuse baptism to the penitent. Nevertheless he is astonished that the last people of whom he would have expected it are availing themselves of the opportunity of salvation which is conferred by baptism performed by him.

That John had baptized in virtue of an authority conferred upon him is testified by Jesus too. On the day after his entry into Jerusalem the scribes ask him by what authority he is acting. They are thinking of how, on the day of his entry, accompanied by his adherents in the caravan from Galilee, he had appeared in the Temple as Lord, had driven the merchants and money-changers from it, and had taught the people that nothing should be done in it which was out of keeping with its purpose of providing a house of prayer for all nations. He promises them a reply to their question if they will first answer his, whether, namely, the baptism of John was from heaven or of men. They dare not deny John an authority proceeding from God, because the people regard him as a prophet. But they are also unwilling to concede it to him, because Jesus could then embarrass them with the counter-question, why had they not believed him? Accordingly they reply, "We do not know". Jesus then considers himself justified in refusing to answer the question by what authority he has acted (Mk. 11 : 15-19, 27-33). Jesus is assuming, therefore, that it was in virtue of the authority he possessed that the baptism of John was efficacious.

It is to the baptism of John that he is referring when he describes the passion and death which are his appointed destiny as the baptism with which he will be baptized. In his reply to the request of James and John that they may sit on his right and left in his glory, he says: "Ye know not what ye ask. Are ye able to drink the cup that I drink? Or to be baptized with the baptism that I am baptized with?" (Mk. 10 : 38). The baptism imparted by John presupposes the idea of being marked for salvation, which is found in Ezekiel (Ezk. 9 : 1–7) and continues to play a part in eschatological expectation.

How did John arrive at the idea of using washing as the means of marking those who were to be saved? It is often assumed that he was led to it by Jewish proselyte baptism or by the kind of lustrations that were common in Hellenistic-oriental mysteries. We know very little about the baptism which those who went over to Judaism received in this period. How could John have adopted for his purposes a usage already common in Judaism? And it is altogether unlikely that the Baptist was influenced by practices from the mystery religions, or even that he knew anything about them or took any interest in them. It is much simpler to suppose that for him the idea of baptism goes back to passages in the prophets in which lustrations efficacious for the removal of sins are promised. Jeremiah and Zechariah both speak of lustrations of this kind to be expected in the future. "O Jerusalem, wash thine heart from wickedness, that thou mayest be saved" (Jer. 4 : 14). "In that day there shall be a fountain opened to the house of David and to the inhabitants of Jerusalem, for sin and for uncleanness" (Zech. 13 : 1). The passage in Ezekiel in which sprinkling with water and the bestowal of the Spirit are mentioned together may have had a special importance for John. "And I will sprinkle clean water upon you, and ye shall be clean: from all your filthiness, and from all your idols, will I cleanse you. A new heart also will I give you, and a new spirit will I put within you. . . ." (Ezk. 36 : 25 f.).

How large a following the Baptist had we do not know. Nor do we know whether he appeared at a time when there was already a strong yearning for the Kingdom of God, or whether it was only his preaching that aroused it. The probability is that because of the short duration of his activity the movement was limited to a relatively small circle.

Was his eschatology that of the scribes, like that found in the Psalms of Solomon and the Apocalypses of Baruch and Ezra, or was it that of the Book of Daniel and the Apocalypse of Enoch? Since we have no record of his view of the final events, there is no way to decide. His opposition to the Pharisees (Mt. 3 : 7) inclines us to suspect that, like Jesus, he accepted not their view but that of Daniel and Enoch. In any case he agrees with Jesus in that he does not regard descent from Abraham as an absolute condition of entering the Kingdom. This is clear from his saying to the Pharisees that they should not rely on being Abraham's offspring, since God could raise up children to Abraham from stones (Mt. 3 : 9).

Jesus himself let John baptize him. As he rose from the water of Jordan he received a vision in which he saw the Spirit descend upon him and heard the voice of God declare that he was his beloved Son (i.e. the Messiah) (Mk. 1 : 9–11). It was therefore at his baptism that he experienced his call to be the Messiah. According to Mark's account (and this probably shows that it is the older), he received his baptism from John without any knowledge on the part of the latter of who he was or what had befallen him at this moment. In Matthew John refuses to baptize him, because he knows that he is higher than himself, and Jesus pacifies him with the remark, "Thus it becometh us to fulfil all righteousness", whereupon he performs it. In many respects, too, the vision to Jesus takes on in this account the character of a miracle experienced by the others present also. The text permits of the inference that they all heard the voice from heaven (Mt. 3 : 13–17). After his baptism Jesus goes into solitude (Mk. 1 : 12). Immediately after the imprisonment of the Baptist he appears in Galilee and preaches, as John had done, that the Kingdom of God is at hand and men must repent (Mk. 1 : 14 f.).

The Greater who is to come. The Messiah? Elijah?

How does the baptism of John effect salvation? Because it is an initiation, in consequence of which the Spirit is imparted to those who have received it by a greater than John, who is to come after him. They are proved to belong to the Kingdom by their possession of the Spirit, and so are called to survive at the Judgement. "And he [John] preached, saying, There cometh after me he that is mightier than I, the latchet of whose shoes I am not worthy to stoop down and unloose. I baptized you with water; but he shall baptize you with the Holy Ghost" (Mk. 1 : 7 f.). According to Matthew, the greater who is to come "shall baptize you with the Holy Ghost and with fire" (Mt. 3 : 11). Here too the simpler account of Mark is probably the older.

But who is this greater than he whom the Baptist is expecting? It has been naïvely assumed from early times that he was thinking of the Messiah, because Jesus, who did follow him, was the Messiah. If, however, we take account of the Messianic expectation of late Judaism, the question is by no means so simple. It is not there supposed that the Messiah will appear in earthly history as a man. There is not a single piece of evidence for this. The idea of the Messiah becoming man is quite outside the range of ideas in late Jewish Messianic expectation. The Messiah is a supernatural figure who will appear in his glory at the coming of the Messianic Kingdom. But before the manifestation of the Messiah, Elijah must come. Like other great religious figures of earlier times, God had taken him to himself in heaven in the form in which he walked on earth (2 Kg. 2 : 11 f.). According to Malachi 4 : 5 f., God will send him back to earth before the Day of Judgement comes, to prepare men for it.[4] Another sign of the imminence of the end of the world will be the outpouring of the Spirit and the occurrence of wonders (Joel 2 : 28-31).

John does not regard himself as Elijah, the forerunner of the Messiah, but only as a prophet. This is also all that he is for the people, the scribes and the disciples of Jesus (Mk. 11 : 32, Mt. 17 : 9-13). He sees himself called to preach the speedy coming of the Kingdom of God, to summon the people to repentance, to baptize the penitent and to prepare them for the next event to occur, the coming of the great figure of the final period (Elijah) and the outpouring of the Spirit. He combines the two last by teaching that the penitent whom he has baptized shall receive

4 On the return of Elijah, see p. 21.

the Spirit through "him who is to come". The greater than he, who is to come after him and baptize with the Spirit, can only be Elijah. The Messiah is a judge and ruler, not a baptizer.

John's Question to Jesus

As Jesus did not appear till after the imprisonment of the Baptist, the latter's only information about him was what he learned of him in prison. The message of this man who is preaching in Galilee is the same as his own. But he is also performing miracles. True, they were not the mighty nature-miracles of which Joel (2 : 30 f.) and his successors had spoken, but only miracles performed on men. All the same, the Baptist concludes from them that the beginning of the final age has arrived.

He therefore asks himself if Jesus is not the greater than himself for whom he has been looking, and sends some of his disciples to him to ask, "Art thou he that cometh, or look we for another?" (Mt. 11 : 2 f.). If we accept Matthew's account of the baptism of Jesus, which has been influenced by a later outlook, and assume that the Baptist had already recognized Jesus as the Messiah, the question from prison has to be taken as meaning that he has begun to doubt the Messiahship of Jesus. By no stretch of the imagination can the wording of the question be made to fit this interpretation. The many sermons in which it has been made to seem regrettable, and yet to some extent understandable, that the Baptist should have begun to waver in his faith in Jesus as the Messiah and should have asked him for a direct Yes or No are far from the point. Jesus can give the Baptist only an ambiguous answer. He cannot let them tell him that he is Elijah who is to come, because that is false. But he does not want to reveal to the messengers that he regards himself as him who is to be manifested at the coming of the Kingdom as the Messiah. This is his secret and he cannot give it away to them.

Accordingly he conveys to them the unsatisfactory message which has caused so much pondering to expositors from the first, and which even strikes the ordinary reader as odd. "And

Jesus answered and said unto them, Go your way and tell John
the things which ye do hear and see; the blind receive their sight,
and the lame walk, the lepers are cleansed, and the deaf hear,
and the dead are raised up, and the poor have good tidings [of
the approach of the Kingdom of God] preached to them. And
blessed is he, whosoever shall find none occasion of stumbling
in me" (Mt. 11 : 4–6). He bids them report to their master the
miracles which have been happening, so that he can infer from
them how close the final events are. John does not need to be told
whom Jesus considers himself to be. Very soon he will be a
witness of his manifestation as Messiah.

The people, however, are informed, after the departure of the
Baptist's messengers, that it is he who is Elijah. "What went ye
out into the wilderness to behold? . . . To see a prophet? Yea, I
say unto you, and much more than a prophet. This is he, of whom
it is written, Behold I send my messenger before thy face, who
shall prepare thy way before thee [Mal. 3 : 1⁵]. . . . For all the
prophets and the law prophesied until John. And if ye are willing
to receive it, this is Elijah, which is to come" (Mt. 11 : 7–14). It is
plain from the words "*This* is Elijah", that Jesus has understood
the Baptist's question, "Art thou he that cometh?" as meaning,
"Are you Elijah?"

Because of his consciousness of being the future Messiah, Jesus
sees in the Baptist Elijah, who must appear before the coming of
the Kingdom and manifestation of the Messiah. He is the only
person who can possibly enter into consideration for the rôle.
For Jesus, therefore, he is Elijah, even though he does not see
himself as this figure and is not thought to be such by the people.
He does not, moreover, fit at all well into the picture of the prince
of the prophets who had once been taken up to God and would
return to earth from heaven at the beginning of the final age. He
was born a man. Because Jesus knows that it will come as a
complete surprise to the people to see Elijah in the Baptist, he
adds to the announcement, "If ye are willing to receive it", by
which he means, "If you can grasp it".

⁵ Malachi 3 : 1 actually reads: "Behold, I send my messenger, and he shall
prepare the way before me" (meaning the speaker, God).

The Ethics of the Sermon on the Mount

Like the Baptist, Jesus sees his task as consisting above all in teaching men the outlook required for participation in the Kingdom and instilling it into them. He, too, is not concerned to give a description of the final events. Whereas, however, the Baptist calls for a new outlook in quite general terms, Jesus expounds its nature in detail. The ideal of the pious had always been to become righteous men, well-pleasing to God, and so assured of eventual entry into the Kingdom. The way to achieve this state was to observe not only the Law, but also the rules which, according to the tradition laid down by the elders, were designed to regulate life in every detail in obedience to the Law. Jesus, however, teaches that this righteousness is not enough, but a higher righteousness, consisting in keeping the spirit of the commandments, is required. Accordingly he lays down in the Sermon on the Mount, delivered at the very beginning of his ministry, the principle, "Except your righteousness shall exceed the righteousness of the scribes and Pharisees, ye shall in no wise enter into the kingdom of heaven" (Mt. 5 : 20).

In the Beatitudes he mentions the qualities which are an indication of inward membership of the Kingdom. "Blessed are the poor in spirit: for theirs is the kingdom of heaven. . . . Blessed are the meek; for they shall inherit the earth. Blessed are they that hunger and thirst after righteousness: for they shall be filled. Blessed are the merciful: for they shall obtain mercy. Blessed are the pure in heart: for they shall see God. Blessed are the peacemakers: for they shall be called sons of God" (Mt. 5 : 3–9). All the promises introduced by the words "For they shall be" mean the same as the first, though each is expressed in its own different way: they refer to participation in the Kingdom. "They shall inherit the earth" is meant to convey that, as once the people of Israel moved into the land of Canaan which God had promised them, so they will have as their dwelling-place the Kingdom of God. In the Kingdom of God the hunger and thirst of the pious for (true) righteousness will find its satisfaction. In the

Kingdom they will see God face to face and be manifested as his children. Those who showed mercy during their lifetime will receive mercy at the Judgement and be granted the privilege of entry into the Kingdom of God. The poor in spirit are those who have retained the simplicity of heart which is necessary in order to understand the message of the coming of the Kingdom, which is hidden from the wise and understanding and revealed to babes (Mt. 11 : 25). In the Sermon on the Mount and other speeches Jesus expounds the nature of the righteousness which is higher than that of the scribes. The Law is not, in his view, concerned with this or that sinful act, but with the thoughts that lead to it. The prohibition of murder includes hatred and the implacable spirit (Mt. 5 : 21–26). That of adultery means that the entertainment of sinful lust is equivalent to the sinful act. In that of perjury we are shown how questionable all oaths are. A simple yes or no ought to be as dependable as any oath. "But let your speech be Yea, yea; Nay, nay: and whatsoever is more than these is of the evil one" (Mt. 5 : 33–37).

Inward and Outward Ethics

Jesus reproaches the scribes and Pharisees with holding to the outward and literal meaning of scripture and the teaching of the elders instead of going for the essential meaning. They on their side take offence at the way in which his disciples perform work on the Sabbath, in plucking ears of corn to appease their hunger (Mt. 12 : 1–8), and he himself breaks the Sabbath by working cures on that day. His view is that to do good on the Sabbath should count as work permissible on the day of rest (Mt. 12 : 9–14).

What makes him really indignant is the way in which they watch his disciples to see how strictly they observe the method of washing their hands before touching food, required if they are not to be guilty of the offence of eating unclean food. He scolds them for seeking to honour God with such man-made commandments. At the same time he teaches the disciples that it is not what goes into the mouth and passes out of the body in the natural way that defiles a man, but evil thoughts coming from the heart (Mt. 15 : 1–20).

Because he is concerned only with the inward side, and the scribes and Pharisees are interested only in the outward, he sees them as the leaders of God's people who do not have the proper standards of right and wrong, who impose unnecessary burdens on men's shoulders, and who prevent them from finding the way to the Kingdom of God. In the terrible speech he delivers against them in Jerusalem he pronounces the final verdict upon them. He leaves out of account all that they had ventured and achieved for the survival of their ancestral faith when the Jewish religion was in danger of secularization under the Seleucid rule, and all that they had ventured and achieved again when the same danger arose once more under the secularist rulers of the Maccabean line. He does not even let it count in their favour that, with all its tendency to overvalue externals, their piety did help to preserve religion[6].

Where the highest ethic was at stake, and readiness to enter the Kingdom of God demanded no less, their ever more detailed emphasis on the customs that formed part of the development of a cultural tradition had become an obstacle. Looking at the arrival of Jesus in the world of late Judaism, we cannot but be deeply moved by the tragedy of this unavoidable conflict between the two types of ethical piety.

The Highest Demands

Even what the scripture permits cannot always, in the view of Jesus, be regarded as the best possible action. It allows a man to dismiss his wife with a letter of divorce. In his opinion it does so only because of the man's hard-heartedness. For the higher form of righteousness the decisive text is: "What therefore God hath joined together, let not man put asunder" (Mt. 19 : 6). Only for the wife's unfaithfulness may the husband divorce her and marry another. If he does it for any other reason, it is he who is com-

[6] On the stand made by the Pharisees for the religion of their fathers, and the sufferings which it brought them, see p. 50f.

mitting adultery (Mt. 5 : 31 f.; 19 : 3–9). Again, the scripture lays down the rule that after a trial in court any man shall suffer as penalty the bodily injury that he has inflicted on another. 'Breach for breach, eye for eye, tooth for tooth" (Lev. 24 : 19–21). When a man is striving after the highest righteousness he must not behave like this, but is required to put up with what has been done to him, whether a blow has been struck or his coat taken or he has been forced to walk a mile to show someone the way. He should not be concerned to demand punishment and restoration, but only to behave in the way required by the highest inward perfection (Mt. 5 : 38–41). Furthermore he must be peaceable in the highest degree in thought as well as deed.

All judging of other people must be renounced, in view of the coming Judgement to which everyone will be subject. The man who thinks he ought to judge another must always ask himself whether he is not seeing the splinter in his brother's eye, while oblivious to the beam in his own eye (Mt. 7 : 1–5). There must be no contempt, even towards those for whom it is quite appropriate in the generally accepted view. When Jesus has called the tax-collector Matthew to be a disciple, he and his disciples sit at table with tax-collectors and sinners. The Pharisees protest. But he answers them: "They that are whole have no need of a physician, but they that are sick. But go ye and learn what this meaneth, I desire mercy, and not sacrifice (Hosea 6 : 6): for I came not to call the righteous, but sinners" (Mt. 9 : 12 f.).

Jesus teaches his followers to apply altogether different standards from the usual ones in evaluating actions. In the Temple he watches the people putting their gifts for the Temple treasury into the appropriate boxes. Many rich people put in a large sum, a poor widow only two small coins. "And he called unto him his disciples, and said unto them, Verily I say unto you, This poor widow cast in more than all they which are casting into the treasury: for they all did cast in of their superfluity; but she of her want did cast in all that she had, even all her living" (Mk. 12 : 41–44).

No limit is permitted to forgiveness. When Peter asks if it is sufficient to forgive his brother seven times, he receives the reply,

"Not seven times, but seventy times seven" (Mt. 18 : 21 f.). In connexion with this question, Jesus goes on to relate the parable of the servant whose master let him off a debt of ten thousand talents. On the way home he meets a fellow-servant who owes him a hundred pence. In spite of his pleading and promise to pay in full, he has him thrown into the debtors' prison, to stay there until the debt is repaid. On learning of this unforgiving procedure. his master treats him in the same way (Mt. 18 : 23–35).

The Ethic of Love

A scribe asks Jesus the question, with which the scribes were much occupied, Which is the greatest, the all-inclusive commandment? The reply of Jesus goes: "The first is, Hear, O Israel; the Lord our God, the Lord is one: and thou shalt love the Lord thy God with all thy heart, and with all thy soul, and with all thy mind, and with all thy strength.[7] The second is this, Thou shalt love thy neighbour as thyself.[8] There is none other commandment greater than these. And the scribe said unto him, Of a truth, Master, thou hast well said that he is one; and there is none other but he: and to love him with all the heart, and with all the understanding, and with all the strength, and to love his neighbour as himself, is much more than all whole burnt offerings and sacrifices. And when Jesus saw that he answered discreetly, he said unto him, Thou art not far from the Kingdom of God" (Mk. 12 : 29–34).

The higher righteousness, however, demands not only love of our neighbour, but also love of our enemy. "Ye have heard that it was said, Thou shalt love thy neighbour, and hate thine enemy: but I say unto you, Love your enemies, and pray for them that persecute you; that ye may be sons of your Father which is in heaven: for he maketh his sun to rise on the evil and the good, and sendeth rain on the just and the unjust" (Mt. 5 : 43–45). Late Jewish ethics had already risen to the idea of the love of enemies. It finds expression in a collection of proverbs dignified

[7] Deut. 6 : 4 f.
[8] Lev. 19 : 18.

with the name of Solomon, which had been accepted among the books of the Old Testament. "Rejoice not when thine enemy falleth, and let not thine heart be glad when he is overthrown" (Prov. 24 : 17). "If thine enemy be hungry, give him bread to eat; and if he be thirsty, give him water to drink: for thou shalt heap coals of fire upon his head" (Prov. 25 : 21 f.). This second saying is quoted by Paul in Romans (Rom. 12 : 20). The reason why the idea of loving of enemies did not have a more widespread influence on the ethics of late Judaism is that it has no place in the Law. It was only with the demand for an ethic that went beyond the Law that the ground was prepared for its development.

Love of foreigners, on the other hand, does find a place in the Law. "And if a stranger sojourn with thee in your land, ye shall not do him wrong. The stranger that sojourneth with you shall be unto you as the homeborn among you, and thou shalt *love* him as thyself; for ye were strangers in the land of Egypt" (Lev. 19 : 33 f.). This passage gives the Jewish Law its title to noble rank. The man who is striving for the higher righteousness of the kind demanded by Jesus must not refuse his neighbour. He must give to him who asks and must not turn away from him who would borrow from him (Mt. 5 : 42).

The entire thought of those who are looking for the Kingdom of God must be directed towards doing God's will. This is the only thing that counts. A resolution of this kind creates a sense of solidarity among men surpassing any other. "Not everyone that saith unto me, Lord, Lord, shall enter into the Kingdom of heaven; but he that doeth the will of my Father which is in heaven" (Mt. 7 : 21). "For whosoever shall do the will of God, the same is my brother, and sister, and mother" (Mk. 3 : 35). To do God's will, which cannot be confined to commandments and prohibitions, but makes its demand on men's hearts as unlimited will to love: this is the profound, spiritual, inward-looking ethic required for entry into the Kingdom. The meaning of the love which is active in the smallest service to others is the theme of that moving speech which was the last Jesus delivered in the Temple. In the Parable of the Talents he makes the servant to whom least was entrusted guilty by default of failing to use it as his master intended. At the conclusion he announces that the verdict which the Son of Man will pronounce at the Judgement will be based on whether love was shown in the smallest matters. "But when the Son of man shall come in his glory, and all the angels with him, then shall he sit on the throne of his glory; and before him shall be gathered all the nations: and he shall separate them one from another, as the shepherd separateth the sheep from the goats: and he shall set the sheep on his right hand, but the goats on the left. Then shall the King say unto them on his right hand, Come, ye blessed of my Father, inherit the Kingdom prepared for you from the foundation of the world: for I was an hungred, and ye gave me meat: I was thirsty, and ye gave me drink: I was a stranger, and ye took me in; naked and ye clothed me: I was sick, and ye visited me: I was in prison, and ye came unto me. Then shall the righteous answer him, saying, Lord, when saw we thee an hungred, and fed thee? Or athirst, and gave thee drink? And when saw we thee a stranger, and took thee in? Or naked, and clothed thee? And when saw we thee sick, or in prison, and came unto thee? And the King shall answer and say unto them, Verily I say unto you, Inasmuch as ye did it unto one of these my brethren, even these least, ye did it unto me" (Mt. 25 : 31–40).

Jesus' View of Man's Ethical Endowment

What kind of human nature is presupposed in the ethics of Jesus? One which is capable in itself of good, if a man is really in earnest about doing it. Even if men are evil in comparison with God, they are still able to give their children good gifts (Mt. 7 : 11). When the rich young man addresses him as "good master", Jesus checks him with the words, "None is good save one, even God" (Mk. 10 : 18). In reply to the young man's question as to what he must do to inherit eternal life, he refers him in the first place to the Commandments, which forbid men to kill, to commit adultery, to steal, to bear false witness, to defraud, to deny father and mother the honour that is their due. The young man answers that he has kept all this from his youth up. Jesus reproves him for his boast that he has done all this. "And Jesus looking upon him loved him, and said unto him, One thing thou lackest: go, sell whatsoever thou hast, and give to the poor, and thou shalt have treasure in heaven: and come, follow me" (Mk. 10 : 17–21).

Jesus assumes that there are righteous men. His answer to those who reproach him for mixing with tax-collectors and sinners is, "I came not to call the righteous, but sinners" (Mt. 9 : 13). He also holds that men can be good, for otherwise he could not say, "The good man out of his good treasure bringeth forth good things: and the evil man out of his evil treasure bringeth forth evil things" (Mt. 12 : 35).

He has even greater trust in men when they are striving after the good. He expects those who are gathered round him listening to the Sermon on the Mount to become a shining light of goodness for others. "Ye are the light of the world. A city set on a hill cannot be hid. Neither do men light a lamp, and put it under the bushel, but on the stand; and it shineth unto all that are in the house. Even so let your light shine before men, that they may see your good works, and glorify your Father which is in heaven" (Mt. 5 : 14–16).

Out of the story of Adam's eating of the forbidden fruit there arose in late Judaism, and passed over into Christianity, the doctrine that this sin continues to be at work in all mankind. So long as the words of scripture still have some validity—and the words which the earliest records of Jesus give us surely stand supreme—no one ought to expect a Christian to regard this doctrine, which was unknown to Jesus, as part of the essence of the Christian faith.[9] Christians must be allowed to think in this matter as Jesus did. Jesus gives us in his speeches an insight into the essential nature of sin which needs no elaboration in the direction of a doctrine of original sin. Belief in this dogmatic view of sin is not the same thing as grasping and experiencing the problem of guilt in all its depth.

---

[9] For the first appearance of this doctrine in the Apocalypses of Baruch and Ezra, see p. 56f.

Does Jesus have a spiritualized view of the Kingdom of God?

What is the view of the Kingdom of God presupposed by the ethics of Jesus? Historical research devoted to the life of Jesus long assumed as self-evident that he interpreted not only ethics, but also the Kingdom of God, in a spiritual way. Scholars were convinced that he rejected the expectation of the Kingdom of God current in the Judaism of his time as too materialistic and taught a more spiritual doctrine, as he did in ethics. It was likewise assumed that he did not feel himself to be the Messiah in the sense in which he was generally expected, but sought to bring the people to see in him a Messiah of a different sort. This was a Messiah who did not come in supernatural form or with supernatural might, but as a man uniquely endowed with the power of the Spirit of God. He founded the ethical Kingdom of God on earth with his preaching and summoned men to join in its realization.

So long as the four Gospels were regarded as equally authentic sources for our knowledge of the ministry and preaching of Jesus. this view was to some extent tenable. For in the Fourth Gospel Jesus does put forward a type of teaching which he opposes to the Jewish as being more spiritual. In the course of time, however, it came to be recognized that this more spiritual teaching of Jesus really related not to his more inward ethics but to the Greek view of the Logos. It was designed to make Christianity acceptable to the Greeks as the true religious knowledge which had been incomprehensible to the Jews.

When, however, the decision became necessary to regard Matthew and Mark as the only real historical sources, it became much more difficult to maintain the view that Jesus had a spiritualized conception of the Kingdom and his Messiahship. The main argument was that he must have had such a conception to correspond with his spiritualized ethics. Solid evidence could be adduced for this view, in so far as certain parables of the Kingdom do admit of the interpretation that they relate to its establishment and growth. Those in question are the following: the Parable of the Sower, whose seed, though much of it falls on unreceptive ground, yet through the rich yield of the seed that fell on the good soil does indicate success (Mt. 13 : 3–9); the Parable of the Tares, which were sown among the wheat by the wicked enemy, but do not prevent the field from still yielding a harvest (Mt. 13 : 24–30); the Parable of the Mustard Seed, which grows into a great tree (Mt. 13 : 31 f.); that of the Leaven, a piece of which leavens the whole dough (Mt. 13 : 33).

The fact that in the two oldest Gospels Jesus does not put forward any doctrine of the Kingdom of God and his Messiahship seemed to reinforce this apparently self-evident view. This silence of his appeared to justify the acceptance of a spiritual view of the Kingdom, corresponding to his ethics, as belonging to his outlook. In reality, however, this was an error. If Jesus had wished to replace the view of the Kingdom and the Messiah current among his hearers with a different one, he would have had to give clear expression to his views, and in doing so would have provided the scribes and Pharisees with plenty of material for controversy.

Jesus' View of the Kingdom is that of late Judaism

Moreover, the silence of the texts on Jesus' view of the Kingdom and the Messiah (whom he identifies with the Son of Man) is by no means complete. From time to time we find in his sayings more or less accidental indications from which it is clear that he takes the late Jewish view for granted. These sayings, scattered through the text of the Gospels, stand out like rocks in the snow-clad mountains, showing black against the prevailing white. These sayings were either ignored completely or deprived of their meaning by being taken as merely symbolic. If they are taken as they stand, and allowed to state what they do state, and considered all together as a unity, it is no longer possible to maintain the position that Jesus had any attitude to the Kingdom and the Messiah other than that of late Judaism.

Passages about the Kingdom of God in the Speeches of Jesus

The disciples are disputing about who will be the greatest in the Kingdom of God. Jesus does not reprove them for this materialistic outlook, but instructs them on the way a man must behave in his earthly existence if he is to qualify for inclusion among the great in the Kingdom (Mt. 18 : 1-4). Nor does he object to Peter's question, what will be the reward of those who have followed him? He promises them that in return in the new world, when the Son of Man sits on the throne of his glory, they shall sit on twelve thrones, judging the twelve tribes of Israel (Mt. 19 : 27 f.). Nor again is he offended that James and John should ask of him the right to occupy the place of honour on either side of him in the Kingdom of God. All he does is to inform them that the granting of these two seats rests not with the Son of Man, but with God alone (Mk. 10 : 35-40).

The Son of Man-Messiah is, according to Jesus, a supernatural being. He appears on the clouds of heaven, surrounded by his angels, when the time for the Kingdom has come. He promises the disciples whom he sends out in haste to the cities of Israel with the news that the Kingdom is at hand that the advent of the Son of Man will take place before they have gone through all these cities (Mt. 10 : 23). When the High Priest asks him whether he is the Christ (the Messiah), the Son of God, he replies, "Henceforth ye shall see the Son of Man sitting at the right hand of power, and coming on the clouds of heaven" (Mt. 26 : 64). The Son of Man, surrounded by his angels, holds judgement over men (the living and the dead), the fallen angels and the Devil, and the angels will carry out his sentences. "The Son of Man shall send forth his angels, and they shall gather out of his Kingdom all things that cause stumbling, and them that do iniquity, and shall cast them into the furnace of fire: there shall be the weeping and gnashing of teeth. Then shall the righteous shine forth as the sun in the Kingdom of their Father" (Mt. 13 : 41-43). "But when the Son of Man shall come in his glory, and all the angels with him, then shall he sit on the throne of his glory: and before him shall be gathered all the nations" (Mt. 25 : 31 f.).

In the Kingdom everyone exists in the supernatural form of those who have risen from the dead. They are in possession of eternal life. The rich young man who asks Jesus what he must do "to inherit eternal life" means by this "to enter the Kingdom". This comes out clearly in the way in which, after his departure, Jesus speaks of how hard it is for a rich man to enter the Kingdom of God (Mk. 10 : 17–23). In the Resurrection (i.e. in the Kingdom of God) the righteous, according to Jesus' reply to the Sadducees, will be "like angels in heaven" (Mk. 12 : 25). As one risen from the dead at the Messianic feast in the Kingdom of God Jesus will again, as at the Last Supper, drink of the fruit of the vine with his disciples, who will likewise be then in the form of those who enjoy eternal life (Mt. 26 : 29). The risen of every generation and every nation will be united at the Messianic feast: "And I say unto you, that many shall come from the east and the west, and shall sit down with Abraham, and Isaac, and Jacob, in the Kingdom of heaven" (Mt. 8 : 11). There is no escaping the conclusion from these passages that Jesus was expecting a completely supernatural Kingdom of God of the kind described in the prophetic writings of the late post-Exilic period (viz. Malachi, Joel, Is. 24–27, Zech. 9–14, Daniel, Enoch).

It is clear from the fact that as a rule he speaks of the Son of Man rather than of the Messiah that his outlook has its closest affinity with the Book of Daniel and the Book of Enoch. It is closest to that of Enoch.[10] Jesus shares with Enoch the peculiar views that it is not God, as in the later post-Exilic prophets and in Daniel, but the Son of Man, assisted by his angels, who holds the Judgement, that the Judgement extends over the fallen angels as well, that there are great and little in the Kingdom of heaven and that the rich must be regarded as lost from the very beginning.

The eschatology of the scribes, as it is preserved for us in the Apocalypses of Baruch and Ezra, distinguishes two Kingdoms, that of the Messiah, which is limited in duration and takes place before the general resurrection of the dead, and the eternal and

---

[10] On the prophetic writings of the late post-Exilic period and the Books of Daniel and Enoch, see p. 30ff. The views of the Book of Enoch are reproduced on p. 44ff.

completely supernatural Kingdom of God, which appears after the resurrection. Jesus, on the other hand, like the prophetic books of the late post-Exilic period and the Books of Daniel and Enoch, knows only the Kingdom which follows upon the resurrection.[11] The expression Kingdom of heaven, which he frequently uses, is identical in meaning with Kingdom of God. It does not indicate that the Kingdom is in heaven, but that it comes to earth from heaven, so that the earth thereby acquires a supernatural perfection.

Why did Jesus adopt the Late Jewish View of the Kingdom?

Jesus' view of the Kingdom of God is therefore that of late Judaism. It follows that his ethics are not the ethics of the Kingdom, but those appropriate to preparation for its coming. The Kingdom, being supernatural, is beyond ethics. Those who have entered it live there as perfect, angel-like beings in a world which is perfect in every respect. As such they cannot sin.

It would have been quite possible for Jesus to transform the idea of the Kingdom of God to correspond with his spiritualized ethics. He has brought to completion the ethics of Amos, Hosea, Jeremiah, Ezekiel and Deutero-Isaiah. The ethical teaching of Deutero-Isaiah in particular has all the appearance of a preliminary draft of his.[12] He could therefore have taken over the view of the Kingdom held by the early prophets, towards which their ethics were oriented. For them the Kingdom is essentially a spiritual and ethical entity. Indeed, it comes into existence when God transforms the hearts of men by imparting to them his Spirit and delegates dominion over all nations to a king of the House of David who has been equipped with the Spirit. In Jeremiah, Ezekiel and Deutero-Isaiah the Kingdom consists in a new everlasting covenant which God makes with his people, by which he gives them the strength to endure through imparting his Spirit to them.

[11] On the distinction between the Messianic Kingdom and the Kingdom of God in the eschatology of the scribes, see p. 59f.

[12] On the ethics of Deutero-Isaiah, see p. 15f.

To be sure, we also find in the early prophets from Isaiah on-ward the expectation that in the age of the Kingdom God will intervene in nature and bestow upon it a harmonious perfection which involves better conditions of living for men. But this does not affect the spiritual and ethical character of the Kingdom. The essential thing about it is that men are enabled by the Spirit to recognize and to do the will of God in a way that was previously impossible.[13] The ethics preached by the earlier prophets not only prepare men for the Kingdom, but are also valid in it when it comes, and indeed make it what it is.

There was nothing to prevent Jesus, who continued and com-pleted the ethics of the earlier prophets, from going back from the late Jewish conception of a completely supernatural and super-ethical Kingdom to the earlier idea of a spiritual and ethical Messianic Kingdom, and giving it new life and depth in accordance with his deeper ethical insight. This is not what he does; instead he accepts the late Jewish view and directs his ethics towards one purpose alone. This is to prepare those who belong to the last generation of mankind, and are prepared to give credence to his message, for entry into the Kingdom, thus making the most of the last moments of the present time order, between his announce-ment of the imminence of the Kingdom and its advent.

There was a good reason for accepting the late Jewish view of the Kingdom. The spiritual and ethical Kingdom of the prophets fails in one respect to provide a satisfactory solution of the problem of God, man and the world. It is only available for the righteous of the last generation of mankind who experience its coming. The righteous of all earlier generations get nothing. All their striving to be well-pleasing to God was in vain. It must therefore be taken for granted that not only the righteous of the last generation, but all who had ever lived, belonged to the Kingdom. There must be faith in the resurrection as well as in the Kingdom.[14] But this meant a fundamental change in the nature of the Kingdom. Those who have risen from the dead

[13] On the spiritual nature of the Kingdom of God in the early prophets, see p. 5ff.

[14] On the rise of belief in the resurrection in Jewish eschatology, see p. 32f.

and men in their natural state (the survivors of the last generation) cannot both be in the Kingdom together. They must all be supernatural beings, the one through the resurrection, the others through a transformation which they will undergo at the appearance of the Kingdom.

The supernatural condition of those who participate in the Kingdom requires the Kingdom itself to be supernatural. There is another reason too why it must be so. The Messianic, spiritual and ethical Kingdom is in another respect as well an unsatisfactory solution of the problem of God, man and the world. When the conception of the Kingdom first developed out of that of the Day of Yahweh in Amos, the God of Israel was concerned only with the gods and kings of the enemies of his people.[15] Later, however, it came to be recognized that he was the only God and that his dominion had to prevail over wicked world powers which were responsible for the evil and wickedness in the world. The Kingdom of God became a new world in which these powers, and death too, no longer prevailed.

This new conception of the Kingdom was higher than the earlier, in that it rested on a deeper insight into the problems presented to the pious and aimed at providing a correspondingly more comprehensive solution. For the later outlook the Messianic Kingdom of the earlier prophets has been to some extent superseded. In the Apocalypses of Baruch and Ezra the theology of the scribes accords it a place corresponding to its changed status. It is now the brief temporary prelude to the Kingdom of God, after which, with the resurrection of the dead, the curtain rises on the event which will last for eternity.[16]

The faith which sets its hopes highest and dares to expect that God will shortly make an end to the present era and bring in the age of perfection can entertain no other view but that of a supernatural and super-ethical Kingdom of God. That is why Jesus adopted the outlook of late Judaism.

[15] On the rise of the conception of the Kingdom of God out of that of the Day of Yahweh, see p. 3f.

[16] On the conception of the Messianic Kingdom and the Kingdom of God in the Apocalypses of Baruch and Ezra, see p. 59f.

The writers of the post-Exilic and late Jewish prophetic books devote themselves to the description of the final events amid which the coming of this Kingdom will take place. They are not concerned with the problem that entry into a supernatural state requires a preparedness belonging to the highest ethics. The cultus had again acquired so much importance for them that they no longer stood by the great achievement of the prophets in seeing the ethical as the only valid standard. Of course Jesus shares the late Jewish view of the Kingdom of God. But he is not really concerned with it. He is working out and proclaiming the conditions necessary for entry into the Kingdom and acceptance as a child of God. The late Jewish view of the Kingdom is the vessel in which his deeper and more spiritual ethic is contained.

Influence of the View of the Kingdom as completely supernatural on the Ethics of Jesus

What bearing does expectation of a supernatural Kingdom have on the ethics of Jesus? It is responsible for a depreciation of the existing transient and imperfect world in comparison with the eternal and perfect world to come. For Jesus this is greatly accentuated by his belief that the time allotted to the present world is now very short indeed. Detachment from all that belongs to this world is therefore essential.

To Jesus the young children of the final human generation are destined to enter the Kingdom as they are. They pass their existence in this world in innocence and freedom from anxiety, and will never know any other way of living here because the Kingdom will have come before they are grown up. They possess a unique privilege. "And they brought unto him little children, that he should touch them: and the disciples rebuked them. But when Jesus saw it, he was moved with indignation, and said unto them, Suffer the little children to come unto me: forbid them not: for of such is the Kingdom of God. Verily I say unto you, Whosoever shall not receive the Kingdom of God as a little child, he shall in no wise enter therein. And he took them in his arms, and blessed them, laying his hands upon them" (Mk. 10 : 13-16).

To feel a need for respect and power and miss the importance of humility during the time of waiting for the Kingdom means a serious entanglement in the affairs of this world. The position in the Kingdom of God is that to have been insignificant in this world is proof of being called to be one of the great in the Kingdom, while to have been one of the great in this world is proof that one is called to be of little account in the Kingdom, if indeed one gets into it at all. The aim at which to strive is therefore not greatness and power, but insignificance and service. "In that hour came the disciples unto Jesus, saying, Who then is greatest in the Kingdom of heaven? And he called to him a little child, and set him in the midst of them, and said, Verily I say unto you, Except ye turn, and become as little children, ye shall in no wise enter into the Kingdom of heaven. Whosoever therefore shall humble himself as this little child, the same is the greatest in the Kingdom of heaven" (Mt. 18 : 1–4). In his reply to the request of James and John to be granted the seats of honour on his right and left, Jesus explains: "Ye know that the rulers of the Gentiles lord it over them, and their great ones exercise authority over them. Not so shall it be among you: but whosoever would become great among you shall be your minister; and whosoever would be first among you shall be your servant" (Mt. 20 : 25–27). Jesus even sees it as a requirement of the times that men who enjoy a position of respect in the spiritual sphere must decline the appropriate titles of honour customarily bestowed upon them. "Be not ye called Rabbi: for one is your teacher, and all ye are brethren. And call no man your father on the earth: for one is your Father, which is in heaven. Neither be ye called masters: for one is your master, even the Christ. But he that is greatest among you shall be your servant. And whosoever shall exalt himself shall be humbled; and whosoever shall humble himself shall be exalted" (Mt. 23 : 8–12).

Another entanglement in the things of this world which is incompatible with expectation of the Kingdom is attachment to one's possessions. Jesus even considers that with the Kingdom so close at hand the earning of one's living has lost its justification. Concern about the necessities of life should now be left entirely to God. "Lay not up for yourselves treasures upon the earth, where moth and rust doth consume, and where thieves break through and steal; but lay up for yourselves treasures in heaven, where neither moth nor rust doth consume, and where thieves do not break through nor steal: for where thy treasure is, there will thy heart be also" (Mt. 6 : 19–21). After the departure of the rich young man, who could not bring himself to follow his advice, selling all his possessions, giving the proceeds to the poor, and following him, Jesus says to the disciples: "How hard is it for them that trust in riches to enter into the Kingdom of God! It is easier for a camel to go through a needle's eye, than for a rich man to enter into the Kingdom of God. And they were astonished exceedingly, saying unto him, Then who can be saved? Jesus looking upon them saith, With men it is impossible, but not with God: for all things are possible with God" (Mk. 10 : 24–27). "Be not therefore anxious, saying, What shall we eat? or, What shall we drink? or, Wherewithal shall we be clothed? For after all these things do the Gentiles seek; for your heavenly Father knoweth that ye have need of all these things. But seek ye first his Kingdom, and his righteousness; and all these things shall be added unto you" (Mt. 6 : 31–33).

Renunciation of Work. Pure Ethic of Perfection

The ethics of Jesus are concerned only with the attainment of inner perfection. They renounce moral works. They have nothing to do with the achievement of anything in the world. His expectation of the supernatural Kingdom of God which is coming in the very near future puts Jesus in a position to disregard everything that ethics can achieve in this world. Their sole function is to make individual men face the need to reflect on the nature of the true good. His ethics can set up the highest, most unlimited demands. The establishment of better conditions in the world does not come into the picture. This means that ethics are delivered from any need to listen to considerations of prudence, which always mean giving way to compromise and accepting the will to the merely relatively good.

The reality with which the ethics of Jesus deal has nothing to do with conditions existing in the world and in human society, but only with those that exist in the hearts of individuals. His ethics do not concern themselves with such a question as whether following out the command not to resist evil may not threaten the existence of relatively well-ordered social conditions.

No system of ethics can be complete unless it calls upon men at one and the same time both for the attainment of inward perfection and for activity. Nevertheless it is of immense importance in the spiritual history of mankind that Jesus made men think only of what they knew in their hearts was the way to become what they were meant to be. We are all constantly in danger of confining ourselves to the relatively valid commands of moral activity and in the process of forgetting the need to strive to become truly moral. Again and again Jesus compels us to look away from what we aim at and achieve in our moral activity and to call ourselves to account for what we really are. Only in proportion to our endeavour to become truly moral are we ready to engage in moral activity in the right way. We must never let our wrestling with the demands of absolute personal ethics slacken into contentment with the modest requirements of the relative and general.

Active Love. Rejection of Asceticism

The way in which Jesus denies life and the world is different from that of India. It is not a denial of existence as such in comparison with non-existence, but rather a renunciation of the present imperfect world in comparison with the perfect world to come. It is not a total, but only a provisional denial of life and the world. With total denial, the only outlook or attitude that comes into the picture is world-renunciation, and there is no longer any place for ethics. It is so imprisoned in complete indifference to everything related to existence that it cannot escape from it. It may pass off complete world-renunciation as ethics: any real ethics are precluded.

Buddha (died c. 480 B.C.), who was a morally sensitive man, tried hard to fit ethics into the total Indian denial of life and the world. Since this excludes all activity, he had to content himself with an ethic purely of thoughts. Only occasionally did he venture to forget about complete denial of life and the world, and succumb to the temptation to let love be active.[17]

Jesus, on the other hand, whose denial of life and the world is only partial, is in a position to call for active ethical behaviour towards our fellow-men, even if he too must renounce systematic ethical activity as being really meaningful. His ethics, like those of late Judaism, come from the life- and world-affirming ethics of the prophets. Both are affected by the fact that in the later post-Exilic period the idea of the Messianic Kingdom as something which will come into existence in this world (an idea arising out of ethical affirmation of life and the world) is replaced by that of the supernatural Kingdom of God. The life- and world-denial which this entailed did not become dominant in the development of Jewish ethics because the supernatural Kingdom was still regarded as something in the remote future.

Jesus, however, expects it to come immediately. For him, consequently, the far-reaching denial of life and the world that goes with this doctrine completely overshadows the spirit of affirmation that underlies his ethic as a continuation of that of the prophets. Great as this influence is, it does not entirely change the nature of his ethic. There remains in it a strain of life- and world-affirmation. Dissociation from the world and active love exist in it side by side. Though in the main it comes down on the side of denial of life and the world, yet it also retains some affinity with the spirit of affirmation.

This continuing influence of life- and world-affirmation explains not only how Jesus can still find a place for ethical activity, but also his rejection of every kind of asceticism. Although he calls for the limitation of desires, his ethic concedes to man everything that belongs to a natural way of living. The claims of marriage are in no way called in question: it is regarded as part

[17] On Buddha's ethics, see Albert Schweitzer, *Indian Thought and its Development*, pp. 100–120.

of God's will. Fasting is not to be accounted necessary: Jesus allows himself and his disciples freedom not to practise it.

There is also a special reason for his rejection of asceticism. It is not this, but only freedom from anxiety, that meets the need of the times. For this is a time of rejoicing. The message has gone forth that the Kingdom of God has been seen to be dawning. Moreover he who will be manifested as the Messiah and Son of Man finds himself unrecognized by those who hear the news. The last generation of mankind enjoys an enormous privilege in being allowed to experience all this. After preaching the Parable of the Sower, Jesus says to the disciples: "Blessed are your eyes, for they see; and your ears, for they hear. For verily I say unto you, that many prophets and righteous men desired to see the things which ye see, and saw them not; and to hear the things which ye hear, and heard them not" (Mt. 13 : 16 f.). It is because this is a time for joy that Jesus and his disciples abstain from fasting. "Then come to him the disciples of John, saying, Why do we and the Pharisees fast oft, but thy disciples fast not? And Jesus said unto them, Can the sons of the bride-chamber mourn, as long as the bridegroom is with them?" (Mt. 9 : 14 f.). Because Jesus eats and drinks like any other man, he has to put up with being called by men a glutton and a drunkard. In the speech in which he reveals to the people that John is more than a prophet, he confirms that both John and he displeased the masses, each by that which distinguished him from the other. "For John came neither eating nor drinking, and they say, He hath a devil. The Son of Man came eating and drinking, and they say, Behold, a gluttonous man, and a winebibber, a friend of publicans and sinners!" (Mt. 11 : 18 f.).

Buddha likewise ascribed value only to detachment from the world, not to asceticism. The good news he brings, which deprives asceticism of all validity, is the revelation that redemption can be enjoyed without the discipline, which was usually deemed to be necessary, of mortifying one's existence by every imaginable kind of self-torture.

4. JESUS' MESSIANIC CONSCIOUSNESS

Jesus did not come forward as Messiah

We are accustomed to regard it as self-evident that Jesus came forward as the Messiah and required those who listened to his preaching to believe in his Messiahship. According to the two oldest Gospels, however, he did not do this. He never tells the masses that he is the Messiah. The believers know nothing of it.

For a very long time, right down to the beginning of the twentieth century, even critical research into the life of Jesus did not accept the fact as it should have done that in the two oldest Gospels Jesus does not appear as Messiah. The view which had always prevailed, that his Messiahship formed part of the content of his preaching, was so deep-rooted that the significance of this special feature of the narrative of Matthew and Mark was not appreciated. Even in Luke the tradition that he did not come forward as Messiah is no longer fully maintained. In the Fourth Gospel it is completely abandoned.

Two facts show irrefutably that Jesus did not come forward as Messiah and did not expect his hearers to believe in him as such. At the entry into Jerusalem the people from the city ask the Galileans who form Jesus' following who it is who is being honoured in this way. They receive the reply, "This is the prophet, Jesus, from Nazareth of Galilee" (Mt. 21 : 10 f.). This means that "Hosanna to the Son of David" and "Blessed is he that cometh in the name of the Lord" (Mt. 21 : 9) apply, however strange it may seem to us, not to the Messiah, but to the prophet from Nazareth.

The second fact is in agreement with the first and confirms it. At the trial the High Priest first tries to convict Jesus on the basis of the evidence of witnesses. Finally he makes two come forward and quote a saying that he is supposed to have uttered against the Temple. Why does he waste time with such unreliable pieces of evidence instead of establishing through witnesses that Jesus claimed to be the Messiah? He cannot, because he does not have at his disposal the three witnesses needed for a conviction according to the Law. True, he has somehow or other learned that

Jesus considers himself the Messiah. But this is of use to him only if Jesus admits it. He therefore gives up the attempt to proceed further with witnesses and turns to Jesus with the words, "I adjure thee by the living God, that thou tell us whether thou be the Christ, the Son of God". Jesus does admit it. Upon this the High Priest, turning to the scribes and elders, says: "He hath spoken blasphemy: what further need have we of witnesses?" Whereupon he is found guilty of a capital offence (Mt. 26 : 59–66).

It never occurs to those listening to Jesus, in spite of the miracles he is working, that he might be the Messiah. In the late Jewish view the Messiah is not to be looked for as a man or as appearing in this world. The Messiah of the prophets was to be born as a man and made Messiah through the bestowal by God of the Spirit. The Messiah of late Judaism, on the other hand, is a supernatural being, because the Kingdom is supernatural. Like the Kingdom, he belongs to the future. True, he is still called David's son, as he was in the prophets. But the late post-Exilic prophets, the Psalms of Solomon, and the Apocalypses of Baruch and Ezra never posed, let alone solved, the question how, as a supernatural being, he could at the same time actually be born as a man, as David's successor.[18]

Jesus expects to be revealed as Messiah at the Coming of the Kingdom of God

The Messianic consciousness of Jesus cannot therefore consist in a belief that he is the Messiah while he is still a man, but only in the view that he is the one who will be revealed as Messiah at the coming of the Kingdom. Along with all who share in the Kingdom, he will receive, when it comes, a supernatural form of existence, and only then will he become Messiah. His Messianic consciousness is of the kind that looks to the future.

The question which those late Jewish scribes who concerned themselves with the coming of the Kingdom and the Messiah dared not ask themselves, because they could find no answer to it, Jesus has solved in the only way possible. He assumes that a man

[18] On the late Jewish conception of the Messiah, see p. 53ff.

born as a descendant of David in the last generation of mankind will be revealed as the Messiah in his supernatural existence at the coming of the Kingdom. He is convinced that he is this descendant of David.

The conviction that he is the future Messiah is a secret that he keeps to himself. His hearers do not need to know that he is more than the herald of the nearness of the Kingdom of God and of the higher righteousness required for entry into it. It is enough for them to believe in the nearness of the Kingdom and to prepare themselves for its coming. They will find out soon enough that he is the Messiah.

His knowledge that he is descended of David's line is therefore a presupposition of Jesus' Messianic consciousness. Others too know of this. The Canaanite woman addresses him as "O Lord, thou Son of David" (Mt. 15 : 22). The blind beggar at Jericho, who hears that Jesus of Nazareth is to pass through, cries to the Son of David in the hope of attracting his compassion (Mk. 10 : 47 f.). This does not mean that he is consciously hailing him as Messiah. Afterwards, when he stands before him, he addresses him as Rabbi (Mk. 10 : 51). The cry of Hosanna at the entry into Jerusalem is meant for the Son of David, whom the Galileans describe to the people of Jerusalem as the prophet Jesus from Nazareth (Mt. 21 : 9–11). The priests and scribes reprove Jesus for taking pleasure in hearing the children sing to him in the Temple, "Hosanna to the Son of David" (Mt. 21 : 15), without having the slightest inkling that this means that he claims to be the Messiah. It is important to note that for Paul too it is an established fact that Jesus "after the flesh" is of David's line (Rom. 1 : 3).

The riddle that Jesus put to the Pharisees in the Temple deals with the Davidic descent of the Messiah. How, he asks them, can David call the Messiah, who as his descendant is subordinate to him, his Lord? He does this in the 110th Psalm, which is ascribed to David and refers to the Messiah. In this Psalm (110 : 1) he says, "The Lord saith unto my Lord [meaning the Messiah], Sit thou at my right hand, until I make thine enemies thy footstool" (Mk. 12 : 35–37). The solution to the riddle is that the

Messiah in his earthly existence is subordinate to David as his successor, but in the coming Kingdom, as the Messiah, he is above him. In this catch question Jesus does not therefore mean, as was so long supposed, to call in question the view that the Messiah must be of David's line. He accepts this as his starting-point, because he is conscious of being both the descendant of David and, at the same time, the future Messiah. Their failure to solve the problem presented by the scripture is intended to make the Pharisees see how defective is their knowledge of the Messiah.

Jesus' View of the Equivalence of the Messiah and the Son of Man

Besides the problem of the Davidic descent of the Messiah, there was for late Judaism yet another: that of the relationship of the Son of Man to the Messiah. The eschatology of the scribes found in the Psalms of Solomon and the Apocalypses of Baruch and Ezra knows only the Messiah, while that of the Book of Daniel and the Book of Enoch knows only the Son of Man.[19] It is a mistake to assume that both designations were used in late Judaism as equivalent in meaning. In point of fact the combination in one figure of the Messiah and the Son of Man is first found in Jesus. This equation, like the idea of the human pre-existence of the Messiah, was a considerable intellectual achievement. What is remarkable is the way in which Jesus used the term Son of Man not only for the supernatural being who comes on the clouds, but also when he is speaking of himself in his earthly existence.

Son of Man means in Aramaic, the language spoken by Jesus, simply man. In Daniel the term denotes the ruler in the Kingdom of God because he is seen by Daniel in a vision as a being of human form, in contrast with the beasts who represent the empires of the world, and the angels.[20]

It is possible that this designation of the ruler of the Kingdom as

---

[19] On the Messiah and the Son of Man in late Jewish eschatology, see pp. 30ff., 46ff., 53ff., 59ff.

[20] On the Son of Man in Daniel, see p. 30ff.

Son of Man, appearing as a parallel to the usual term Messiah, helped Jesus to realize that the Messiah might first have to go through existence as a man. He may have found hidden in this strange expression for the Messiah the secret that the expected supernatural Messiah must also be born as son of a man. When Jesus uses the term Son of Man to describe himself, he does not mean that he is an incarnation of a pre-existent being, but that he is the man of David's line who will be the Son of Man in the Kingdom of God.

Whether the Son of Man is a pre-existent heavenly being for Daniel is not altogether clear. The Book of Enoch certainly takes this view of him[21] (En. 48 : 2–7). This does not mean that Jesus, whose view of the Messiahship presupposes a previous human existence of the Son of Man, also ascribed to him heavenly pre-existence. It is probable that he inclined to the view that a normal son of man selected for the office by God will become a heavenly being on the advent of the Kingdom.

Even if he did regard the Son of Man as a pre-existent heavenly being, he certainly did not consider himself an incarnation of this being. The need for this difficult concept of a heavenly being dwelling in a man only arose at the time when it was held that Jesus was already Messiah during his earthly existence. Where, as with Jesus, the eschatological point of view still prevailed that the Messiah, like the Kingdom, belonged to the future, the two figures are thought of as coming in succession, not simultaneously. Accordingly, Jesus did not assume that he was both man and this pre-existent heavenly being in one, but saw himself as the man in whom this being had to undergo a completely human existence before beginning his reign in the Kingdom. From the eschatological point of view the humanity of the Messiah-Son of Man, if such a being is envisaged at all, is the result not of an incarnation, but of a temporary renunciation of his heavenly form of existence in order to enter into an entirely human one.

Through his double use of the term Son of Man Jesus demonstrates that he and the Son of Man who will one day appear from heaven somehow belong together. Here he is giving away

21 On the Son of Man in Enoch, see p. 46.

something of his Messianic secret. He need not, however, have any fear that it will be understood. It is well protected. The idea that the expected Son of Man will have a human before his heavenly existence is one that never occurs to his hearers.

Disclosure of the Secret of his future Messiahship in Jesus' Teaching and Action

His Messianic consciousness quite often comes to light in the teaching and activity of Jesus. He claims to be able to forgive sins on earth (Mk. 2 : 10) and to be lord of the Sabbath (Mk. 2 : 28). He asserts that he is more than the prophet Jonah (Mt. 12 : 41). Whether one will be saved or lost depends on the relation in which one stands to him. Those whom he does not acknowledge at the Judgement are condemned (Mt. 7 : 21-23). In the Sermon on the Mount he declares those blessed who are persecuted for his sake (Mt. 5 : 11 f.). He will intercede with his heavenly Father for those who acknowledge him (Mt. 10 : 32). He insists that men must bring themselves to love him more than father or mother, and have the determination to follow him in his suffering (Mt. 10 : 37 f.). "And every one that hath left houses, or brethren, or sisters, or father, or mother, or children, or lands, for my name's sake, shall receive a hundredfold, and shall inherit eternal life" (Mt. 19 : 29). It will be worse on the Day of Judgement for the city which does not receive his disciples than for Sodom and Gomorrah (Mt. 10 : 14 f.). Fellowship, not only directly with him, but also with those who belong to him, is effective for salvation. "He that receiveth you [the disciples] receiveth me, and he that receiveth me receiveth him that sent me" (Mt. 10 : 40). "And whosoever shall give to drink unto one of these little ones a cup of cold water only, in the name of a disciple, verily I say unto you, he shall in no wise lose his reward" (Mt. 10 : 42). On the Day of Judgement men will enter the Kingdom according to the verdict of the Son of Man, given on the ground that they did good in the hour of need to those in whom they did not know that they were looking on their brothers (Mt. 25 : 31-40).

Of the Baptist Jesus says that he is Elijah, although neither he nor the people thought of him as such. But if Elijah has already come, he himself can only be the future Messiah (Mt. 11 : 14). He enters Jersualem riding upon an ass, in order that the Messianic prophecy of Zech. 9 : 9, "Tell ye the daughter of Zion, Behold, thy king cometh unto thee, meek, and riding upon an ass, and upon a colt the foal of an ass", may be fulfilled (Mt. 21 : 1–9). For everyone else he enters as the prophet from Nazareth of David's line. But for himself it is the entry of the future Messiah.

He carries out the cleansing of the Temple with the authority he assumes as the coming Son of Man. He is probably acting on the basis of the closing words of the prophetic Book of Zechariah: "In that day [he means the day on which Jerusalem will be completely holy unto Yahweh] there shall be no more a trafficker [R.V. margin] in the house of the Lord of hosts" (Zech. 14 : 21). From the day of his triumphal entry until his arrest he conducts himself as lord of the Temple.

The only danger to Jesus' Messianic secret comes from the demons. They address him as "Son of God". In the synagogue at Capernaum one of them cries out: "What have we to do with thee, thou Jesus of Nazareth? Art thou come to destroy us? I know thee who thou art, the Holy One of God" (Mk. 1 : 24). Similar outcries are heard from a demoniac in the land of the Gerasenes (Mk. 5 : 1–8) and in other places. "And the unclean spirits, whensoever they beheld him, fell down before him, and cried, saying, Thou art the Son of God. And he charged them much that they should not make him known" (Mk. 3 : 11 f.). Even their cries do not suggest to the people that he might be the future Messiah.

The Disciples become aware of Jesus' Messianic Secret

The disciples, however, did come into possession of the secret. In the neighbourhood of Caesarea Philippi (on the southern slopes of the mountain in which the Jordan rises), to which Jesus had withdrawn with them so as not to be constantly surrounded by the people, as he was on the shore of the Sea of Galilee, he asks them whom they consider him to be. He learns from Peter that he is aware of his Messiahship. "Now when Jesus came into the parts of Caesarea Philippi, he asked his disciples, saying. Who do men say that the Son of Man is? And they said, Some say John the Baptist; some, Elijah: and others, Jeremiah, or one of the prophets. He saith unto them, But who say ye that I am? And Simon Peter answered and said, Thou art the Christ, the Son of the living God. And Jesus answered and said unto him, Blessed art thou, Simon Bar-Jonah: for flesh and blood hath not revealed it unto thee, but my Father which is in heaven. . . . Then charged he the disciples that they should tell no man that he was the Christ" (Mt. 16 : 13–17, 20). In Jesus' view, therefore, Peter did not arrive at the secret by himself: it was revealed to him by God. How and when did this occur?

We cannot reject out of hand the possibility that it was at the event generally called the Transfiguration. "And after six days Jesus taketh with him Peter, and James, and John his brother, and bringeth them up into a high mountain apart: and he was transfigured before them: and his face did shine as the sun, and his garments became white as the light. And behold, there appeared unto them Moses and Elijah talking with him. And Peter answered, and said unto Jesus, Lord, it is good for us to be here: if thou wilt, I will make here three tabernacles; one for thee, and one for Moses, and one for Elijah. While he was yet speaking, behold, a bright cloud overshadowed them: and behold, a voice out of the cloud, saying, This is my beloved Son, in whom I am well pleased; hear ye him. And when the disciples heard it, they fell on their face, and were sore afraid. And Jesus came and touched them and said, Arise, and be not afraid. And lifting up their eyes, they saw no one, save Jesus only.

And as they were coming down from the mountain, Jesus commanded them, saying, Tell the vision to no man, until the Son of Man be risen from the dead. And his disciples asked him, saying, Why then say the scribes that Elijah must first come? And he answered and said, Elijah indeed cometh, and shall restore all things: but I say unto you, that Elijah is come already, and they knew him not, but did unto him whatsoever they listed. Even so

shall the Son of Man also suffer of them. Then understood the
disciples that he spake unto them of John the Baptist"
(Mt. 17 : 1–13). Together with James and John, Peter in his
ecstasy beholds Jesus in a heavenly light and hears the voice from
the cloud saying that he is the Son of God, i.e. the Messiah.

The account of the ecstatic experience follows that of Peter's
confession. It includes, however, statements that make it probable
that it really belongs to a time before it. In that case it would
have been through the revelation he obtained in this ecstatic
experience on the Mount of Transfiguration that Peter acquired
the knowledge of Jesus' Messiahship of which he makes use in his
reply to Jesus at Caesarea Philippi.

It is curious that, on the way down from the mountain, the three
disciples are led by the saying of Jesus about his resurrection to
ask how his resurrection can occur before the coming of Elijah,
since it is only possible after that. There is this justification for the
question, that they do not know that Elijah has already come in
John the Baptist. When Jesus announced this to the people after
the Baptist's inquiry, they were not present; they were on the
missionary journey. Nevertheless the question is remarkable,
because the disciples have heard Jesus' statement about his
resurrection shortly before this at Caesarea Philippi, without
asking then for an explanation of how it could occur before the
coming of Elijah. This favours the view that they first heard
Jesus speak of his resurrection on the descent from the Mount of
Transfiguration, and not at Caesarea Philippi.

It is also difficult to understand how the Transfiguration could
have occurred in the neighbourhood of Caesarea Philippi. It is
presupposed that at the foot of the mountain there is a crowd of
people waiting for Jesus. The narrative testifies to this in the words:
"And when they were come to the multitude, there came to
him a man, kneeling to him" (Mt. 17 : 14). How could the people
be present in this remote neighbourhood at the foot of Mount
Hermon, which Jesus has deliberately sought out in order to be
alone with his disciples?

Jesus is surrounded by the people on the shores of the Sea of
Galilee, particularly at the time of the disciples' missionary

journey and after their return. Immediately after the account of Peter's reply to Jesus at Caesarea Philippi we are told, "And he called unto him the multitude with his disciples" (Mk. 8 : 34). From here on down to Mark 9 : 29 the presence of the crowd is taken for granted. We must also assume that what is related in this section belongs to the time when Jesus was still on the shores of the Sea of Galilee, before he retired to Caesarea Philippi. In that case the vision on the Mount of Transfiguration will have taken place before Peter's confession. However this may be, Peter possesses the knowledge of Jesus' Messianic secret. Through him it is communicated to the disciples at Caesarea Philippi. Jesus strictly forbids them to speak about it. Every time that he speaks of his death and resurrection he impresses this upon them afresh.

How, then, does the High Priest come to know of it? Through the betrayal of Judas. Men have always pondered on why Judas betrayed his master. The main question for historical investigation, however, is what he really betrayed. The betrayal cannot have consisted in giving away the most convenient location for Jesus' arrest. That he went each evening to Bethany could easily have been found out from spies. At the arrest Judas was needed only to enable the soldiers to recognize clearly in the dark the man they were to seize. What concerned the High Priest and the elders of the people first and foremost was to find something that would enable them to proceed against him and put him out of the way. Judas gave it to them. Only from someone in the circle of disciples could they have learned that Jesus thought of himself as the coming Messiah. His admission of it when questioned by the High Priest made it possible to sentence him to death without bringing in three witnesses to it.

5. THE SECRET OF JESUS' PASSION

It was not failure that drove Jesus to go to his Death

Immediately after the disciples have learned from Peter that Jesus is the coming Messiah, he announces to them that he must die and will rise again. "From that time began Jesus to shew unto his disciples, how that he must go unto Jerusalem, and suffer many things of the elders and chief priests and scribes, and be killed, and the third day be raised up" (Mt. 16 : 21). On the journey to Jerusalem he repeats this announcement (Mt. 17 : 22 f.; 20 : 17–19). There are two passages in which he speaks to them about the meaning of his death, though only indirectly. When he teaches them that he who would be great in the Kingdom of God must be a servant here on earth, he concludes with the words, "even as the Son of Man came not to be ministered unto, but to minister, and to give his life a ransom for many" (Mt. 20 : 28). At the Last Supper he passes round the cup with the words, "This is my blood of the covenant, which is shed for many" (Mk. 14 : 24).[22] Thus Jesus lets the disciples know that he must die. But he never explains to them the necessity and meaning of his death. He contents himself with saying to them that it will be to the benefit of many.

How are we to explain the origin of the resolve to go to his death and the meaning of this self-sacrifice? For many years historical scholarship held the view that Jesus had come to recognize the necessity for his death as increasing opposition made his work for the Kingdom of God impossible, so that there was no question now of anything but dying for it.[23] This interpretation explains nothing. It does not help anyone to understand in what way Jesus' death benefits others or could help the cause of the Kingdom at all. Moreover there is no foundation for it. The two oldest Gospels know nothing of any theory that in the second period of his mission Jesus had to give way to his opponents. It was not a beaten man who entered Jerusalem amid cries of Hosanna and, sustained by the enthusiasm of the Galilean pilgrims to the feast, could behave for days on end as lord of the Temple.

[22] In Matthew this runs: "which is shed for many unto remission of sins" (Mt. 26 : 28). Since in all the other passages Matthew makes Jesus speak in quite general terms about a ransom for many, in just the same way as he does in Mark, we may assume that Mark is right when in his Gospel Jesus makes only a general reference at the passing round of the cup.

[23] See p. 89f.

The same conclusion emerges from the way in which the High Priest and elders set about getting rid of him. They were perfectly free, so far as the Law went, to have him stoned for his religious offences. There was no need for them to have him condemned by the governor as an agitator and crucified. Why did they not stone him?

Because they had the right, but not the power that was needed. The masses, who honoured him as a prophet, would not have allowed it. That was why they had to arrest him at night, condemn him at a night session (which was illegal), bring him before Pilate and through him have the sentence confirmed and immediately carried out. The crowd which shouted "Crucify, crucify" was not that which had cried "Hosanna", but a group collected at dawn by his accusers. Jesus must hang on the cross and die before his devoted Galileans had even heard of his arrest. That is the explanation of the fact that Jesus was not stoned but crucified.

That he was unable to make headway against an opposition to him which had grown up in Galilee simply does not fit the facts. The only truth behind it is that after the return of the disciples he left Galilee for a time. Why? So as not to be surrounded by the people, but to have only the disciples around him.

At first he tries to escape from the people in the neighbourhood of the Sea of Galilee by moving from place to place by ship at night (Mk. 6 : 30-33, 45-56). He does not succeed: they still flock to him. Then he withdraws to the Gentile neighbourhood of Tyre and Sidon (Mk. 7 : 24-30). From here he returns to Galilee. At first he remains, still surrounded by the people, on the eastern shore in the district of the ten cities (Mk. 7 : 31-8; 9). Then he crosses to the western shore, in the neighbourhood of Dalmanutha, where people again gather round him (Mk. 8 : 10-26). He then retires to the north to the neighbourhood of Caesarea Philippi (Mk. 8 : 27-33).[24] From here he returns to Galilee. He crosses it, in order to make his way to Jerusalem. "And they went forth from thence, and passed through Galilee;

[24] From the north shore of the Sea of Galilee to Tyre is about 40 miles, to Caesarea Philippi about 30.

and he would not that any man should know it" (Mk. 9 : 30). Afterwards, where the road to Jerusalem, in order to avoid Samaria, runs on the east bank of the Jordan, he overtakes, or is overtaken by, the Galilean pilgrim caravan on its way to the feast. "And he arose from thence, and cometh into the borders of Judaea and beyond Jordan: and multitudes come together unto him again" (Mk. 10 : 1). This ever-growing crowd then enters Jerusalem with him.

It is therefore not true that Jesus withdrew from Galilee into the neighbourhoods of Tyre and Caesarea Philippi because the people, stirred up by the scribes, were turning away from him. In reality he left Galilee in order to be alone with the disciples. He wanted to give up preaching for a time. Immediately after the return of the disciples he had announced his intention of being alone with them. "And the apostles gather themselves together unto Jesus; and they told him all things, whatsoever they had done, and whatsoever they had taught. And he saith unto them, Come ye yourselves apart into a desert place, and rest a while. For there were many coming and going, and they had no leisure so much as to eat. And they went away in the boat to a desert place apart. And the people saw them going, and many knew them, and they ran there together on foot from all the cities, and outwent them" (Mk. 6 : 30–33).

Far too little attention has been paid to the fact that the disciples have not fully carried out the commission they received from Jesus. He sent them to the lost sheep of the house of Israel to visit the cities of Israel (Mt. 10 : 6, 23). This included the cities of Judaea, not excepting Jerusalem. It is clear from the fact that he forbids them to go into Gentile territory or the cities of Samaria that he expected their journey to extend beyond Galilee. In what directions and how far they went in pairs is not recorded. At any rate they do not seem to have proclaimed their message in Judaea and Jerusalem. We get the impression that they were not absent very long.

The Delay in the pre-Messianic Tribulation and in the Appearance of the Son of Man

Why does Jesus leave off his preaching after the return of the disciples in order to be alone with them? What has happened? The prospect he held out to the disciples in his speech as he sent them out has not been fulfilled. He told them to proclaim that the Kingdom had begun to dawn and promised them that the Son of Man would come before they had finished with the cities of Israel. "And as ye go, preach, saying, The Kingdom of heaven is at hand. . . . Verily I say unto you, Ye shall not have gone through the cities of Israel, till the Son of Man be come" (Mt. 10 : 7, 23). What he had expected did not occur. In the speech delivered as he sent them out he also held out the prospect of grave persecutions which they would have to endure. "Behold, I send you forth as sheep in the midst of wolves: be ye therefore wise as serpents, and harmless as doves. But beware of men: for they will deliver you up to councils, and in their synagogues they will scourge you; yea and before governors and kings shall ye be brought for my sake, for a testimony to them and to the Gentiles" (Mt. 10 : 16–18). The disciples, however, return to Jesus without a hair of their head having been touched.

What kind of unexpected persecution, coming like a bolt from the blue, was this, for which he thought it necessary to prepare the disciples? It was the pre-Messianic tribulation. According to late Jewish eschatology this, like the appearance of Elijah, was to precede the coming of the Kingdom. It is the beginning of the final events.[25] Anyone proclaiming the approach of the Kingdom must also expect the occurrence of the pre-Messianic tribulation and would have to hold out the prospect of it in his preaching. That is why from the very beginning, even in the Sermon on the Mount, Jesus speaks of persecutions for which believers must be ready.

If he who is to be revealed as Messiah at the coming of the Kingdom is already on earth, walking unrecognized as a man among those who are waiting for its appearance, the question

[25] On the final tribulation, see p. 29f.

inevitably arises, what will happen to him in the pre-Messianic tribulation? Jesus expects that he will have to live through it along with the faithful. In his view the persecution will range about him as the future Son of Man-Messiah. The faithful assembled around him will be particularly assailed by it. For the evil powers of the world, which vent their fury for the last time in the pre-Messianic tribulation, will be looking out for those who belong to God and who are delivered up to them for a time.

Jesus expects, then, to have to endure humiliation before he is revealed as the Messiah. Accordingly he not only informs his followers that they will suffer persecution for his sake, but calls upon them to stand by him in his humiliation and not to doubt him, on peril of forfeiting their entry into the Kingdom. Jesus' conception of the pre-Messianic tribulation differs from the traditional view in two respects. Not only does the Messiah in his human pre-existence have to live through it along with the faithful, but he also assumes that it may be ordained that those who are called to the Kingdom will meet their death in the tribulation.

The traditional view of the tribulation is completely dominated by the idea of testing, which comes from Ezekiel. According to this the righteous have nothing to fear but persecution. They can rest assured that they will not be touched by the slaughter which takes place in the pre-Messianic tribulation. The wicked will be cut off by it. The righteous, on the other hand, remain alive to see the coming of the Kingdom of God and to enter into it.[26] The Apocalypse of Enoch, whose eschatology is so completely different from that of the later prophets and that of the late Jewish scribes (as recorded in the Apocalypses of Baruch and Ezra), shares with them the idea of the testing of the righteous in the pre-Messianic tribulation. It is through the testing that the privilege of the last generation of men in experiencing the coming of the Kingdom of God is ratified.

Jesus demands of his followers that they shall be willing not only to suffer in the tribulation but also, if need be, to give up this temporal life in order to participate in that which is eternal. As

[26] On the view of the testing which comes from Ezekiel, see p. 12.

men risen from the dead, they will enter the Kingdom along with the risen righteous of former generations, in company also with those who have remained alive through the tribulation and have been transformed into a supernatural form of existence.

When Jesus holds out to believers from the very beginning the prospect of severe persecutions in which they must acknowledge him, even if it means their death, he is not therefore thinking of hostility arising from natural, foreseeable causes. He is thinking of the hostility involved in the pre-Messianic tribulation, which is part of the series of events at the end of the world. In his expectation of the pre-Messianic tribulation the thought of suffering, and possibly also death, is in Jesus' mind from the very beginning.

Even in the Sermon on the Mount he speaks of persecutions which the righteous will have to suffer for his sake. "Blessed are they that have been persecuted for righteousness' sake: for theirs is the Kingdom of heaven. Blessed are ye when men shall reproach you, and persecute you, and say all manner of evil against you falsely, for my sake. Rejoice, and be exceeding glad: for great is your reward in heaven: for so persecuted they the prophets which were before you" (Mt. 5 : 10–12). In the mission charge to the disciples it is made perfectly clear that he is thinking of persecutions in the pre-Messianic tribulation. When it is over the appearance of the Son of Man will take place.

Jesus never speaks of the astonishing occurrences which, according to the traditional view, will take place in nature during the tribulation. He does, however, refer to the spiritual aberration in which the closest kinsfolk will proceed against each other with incomprehensible and merciless fury. Jesus' description of this terrible event is in close agreement with that found in the Book of Enoch (En. 100 : 1 f.). "And brother shall deliver up brother to death, and the father his child: and children shall rise up against their parents, and cause them to be put to death. And ye shall be hated of all men for my name's sake: but he that endureth to the end, the same shall be saved. But when they persecute you in this city, flee into the next: for verily I say unto you, Ye shall not have gone through the cities of Israel, till the Son of Man be come. . . . And be not afraid of them which kill the body, but are not able to kill the soul: but rather fear him which is able to destroy both soul and body in hell. . . . Every one therefore who shall confess me before men, him will I also confess before my Father which is in heaven. But whosoever shall deny me before men, him will I also deny before my Father which is in heaven.

Think not that I came to send peace on the earth: I came not to send peace, but a sword. For I came to set a man at variance against his father, and the daughter against her mother, and the daughter in law against her mother in law: and a man's foes shall be they of his own household. He that loveth father or mother more than me is not worthy of me; and he that loveth son or daughter more than me is not worthy of me. . . . He that findeth his life shall lose it; and he that loseth his life for my sake shall find it" (Mt. 10 : 21–39).

Only if we bear in mind that Jesus is expecting the pre-Messianic tribulation and the humiliation which may fall to his lot in it, can we clearly comprehend the meaning of the saying, "Blessed is he, whosoever shall find none occasion of stumbling in me" (Mt. 11 : 6), with which he concludes his message to the Baptist. The Baptist's question, indeed, came while the disciples were on their missionary journey, during which they had been warned to be on the alert for the appearance of the tribulation.

One thing comes out clearly in the mission charge to the disciples. Before Jesus revealed to them at Caesarea Philippi that he must suffer and die in Jerusalem, he had already called upon them and all believers to be ready to suffer with him. Since the scholars who applied themselves to the study of the life of Jesus held this to be incredible, it was assumed that this speech must be a later compilation from sayings of Jesus, including some from the time when he went up to Jerusalem to his death.

The Petition in the Lord's Prayer for Deliverance
from the pre-Messianic Tribulation

It is not only in the assumption that the righteous may suffer death and that the future Messiah may have to live through it along with the faithful that Jesus' view of the pre-Messianic tribulation differs from the traditional view. He also deems it possible that it may be God's will to spare the faithful the need to prove themselves, with the attendant danger that they may fail to pass the test. He teaches them to beg God to do this. Where? In the two last petitions of the Lord's Prayer (Mt. 6 : 13).

The last petition but one, as commonly understood, implies the view that God is men's tempter. We do not fully appreciate the offensiveness of this, because we give the petition the general meaning that he is asked to preserve us from temptation. But this is exegesis, not the original meaning. Literally it speaks of an actual leading by God into temptation: $\mu\dot{\eta}\ \varepsilon\dot{\iota}\sigma\varepsilon\nu\dot{\varepsilon}\gamma\varkappa\eta\varsigma\ \dot{\eta}\mu\tilde{\alpha}\varsigma\ \varepsilon\dot{\iota}\varsigma$ $\pi\varepsilon\iota\varrho\alpha\sigma\mu\acute{o}\nu$. Likewise "deliver" us from evil in the last petition is a very free translation; $\dot{\varrho}\tilde{\upsilon}\sigma\alpha\iota\ \dot{\eta}\mu\tilde{\alpha}\varsigma\ \dot{\alpha}\pi\grave{o}\ \tau o\tilde{\upsilon}\ \pi o\nu\eta\varrho o\tilde{\upsilon}$ means "rescue us from the evil one". It should be noted that the reference is not to the evil which entices us, but to the evil one, thought of personally, the prince of the evil world powers, the Devil.

The two closely connected petitions become intelligible in their true and original sense only when we understand by the *peirasmos* ($\pi\varepsilon\iota\varrho\alpha\sigma\mu\acute{o}\varsigma$) not any sort of temptation to evil to which men may be exposed, but the testing which believers have to undergo in the pre-Messianic tribulation. Jesus bids them pray that God may not lead them into this (i.e. make them undergo it), but that he may rescue them from the evil powers to which they are to be delivered up for a time in the tribulation. He is to make an end of the rule of these powers and to let the Kingdom appear without a prior occurrence of the pre-Messianic tribulation. What has been foreseen as the first occurrence in the scheme of events at the end of the world is to be omitted.

Cancellation of the pre-Messianic Tribulation because of the voluntary Passion and Death of Jesus

Because of the delay in the tribulation the prospect of which he had held out to the disciples when he sent them out on their mission, Jesus came to the conclusion that God was willing to spare believers from it if he fulfilled it in his own person. This he would accomplish by voluntarily undergoing death and so bringing about that end of the domination of evil which was to mark the conclusion of the tribulation.

The many for whom his death is thus a ransom are the righteous of the last generation of mankind, who are to find a place in the Kingdom. According to this view of the meaning of his death, Jesus dies only for them, not for all men. There was never any question of the righteous dead of former generations having to undergo the tribulation. They enter the Kingdom through the resurrection, without any further ado. Jesus is not thinking of future generations, since he holds that the end of time has come.

The death of the Baptist, whom he considered to be Elijah, must have made a great impression on Jesus. It took place while the disciples were on their missionary journey, or soon afterwards. Not long after he received Jesus' reply to the question he had put to him from prison, if not indeed before he received it, the Baptist was beheaded. On the descent from the Mount of Transfiguration Jesus says to the three disciples that he too must die, like the Baptist. "Elijah is come already, and they knew him not, but did unto him whatsoever they listed. Even so shall the Son of Man also suffer of them" (Mt. 17:12). In none of the passages which speak of his coming is there any expectation that Elijah will have to die when he comes back in the final age. According to the account in Mark, Jesus says that the Baptist has suffered death "even as it is written of him" (Mk. 9 : 13). What passage of scripture he can have had in mind is not at all clear.

The fact that the Baptist did not suffer death in the pre-Messianic tribulation, but through a purely human plot, confirms Jesus in his conviction that a similar fate is in store for himself. At the same time he finds this too foretold in the scriptures, as is shown by a remark made at the Last Supper and another at his arrest. After announcing at the Last Supper that one of his own will betray him, he adds: "The Son of Man goeth, even as it is written of him: but woe unto that man through whom the Son of Man is betrayed!" (Mt. 26 : 24). He reproves the disciple who draws his sword at his arrest to defend him with the words: "Thinkest thou that I cannot beseech my Father, and he shall even now send me more than twelve legions of angels? How then should the scriptures be fulfilled, that thus it must be?" (Mt. 26 : 53 f.). There is, however, nothing in the Old Testament about the suffering and death of the Messiah. There could not be anything about it there. In the Old Testament the Messiah is a being for whom suffering and death could never be considered. Jesus too does not expect to suffer and die as the Messiah, but only as the future Messiah, who has been sojourning unrecognized as a man among men. The scripture could have spoken of this only as a secret, applying to the death of the future Son of Man-Messiah while he was walking unrecognized among men: *it could not possibly name him.* It is possible that Jesus did find his death foretold in the obscure passage in Deutero-Zechariah in which the people of Jerusalem lament one who has been killed in their city. "And I will pour upon the house of David, and upon the inhabitants of Jerusalem, the spirit of grace and of supplication; and they shall look unto me whom they have pierced: and they shall mourn for him, as one mourneth for his only son, and shall be in bitterness for him" (Zech. 12 : 10).

That Jesus had noted this passage and interpreted it of his death is rendered probable by the fact that he refers to sayings from Deutero-Zechariah elsewhere. In one of them he finds the challenge to cleanse the Temple (Zech. 14 : 21), in another the allusion which makes him decide to enter Jerusalem as the future Messiah riding upon an ass (Zech. 9 : 9), in a third the suggestion that on the way to his death he will be deserted by his followers (Zech. 13 : 7).[27]

Jesus finds the necessity for his Death foretold in Isaiah 53

He doubtless found the clearest prophecy of his death in the passages of Deutero-Isaiah which deal with the Servant of the

[27] "And in that day there shall be no more a trafficker [R.V. margin] in the house of the Lord of hosts" (Zech. 14: 21). "Shout, O daughter of Jerusalem: behold they king cometh unto thee: he is just, and having salvation; lowly, and riding upon an ass" (Zech. 9 : 9). "I will smite the shepherd, and the sheep of the flock shall be scattered abroad" (Mt. 26 : 31; Zech. 13 : 7).

Lord, whose suffering is of benefit to those who witness it though they do not know it. "He was despised, and rejected of men; a man of sorrows, and acquainted with grief. . . . Surely he hath borne our griefs, and carried our sorrows: yet we did esteem him stricken, smitten of God, and afflicted. But he was wounded for our transgressions, he was bruised for our iniquities: the chastisement of our peace was upon him; and with his stripes we are healed. All we like sheep have gone astray; we have turned every one to his own way; and the Lord hath laid on him the iniquity of us all" (Is. 53 : 3–6).

In their original meaning this and all the other passages about the suffering Servant of God refer to God's people. Their dispersion among the Gentiles, and all the distress that this has meant, serve to bring home to these nations the knowledge of the true God, and so make it possible for them to be converted to him and to share in his glorious Kingdom to come.[28]

That Jesus finds the significance of his suffering and death foretold in the Servant passages is shown by the fact that he speaks of this as the act of service for which the Son of Man has come into the world (Mk. 10 : 45). He is also referring to the Servant passages when he speaks of his death as of benefit to "many", and when he persists in remaining silent before his judges, a silence from which he departs only in order to make a brief acknowledgement to the High Priest that he is the Messiah and to Pilate that he is the king of the Jews. "By his knowledge shall my righteous servant justify many" (Is. 53 : 11). "He was oppressed, yet he humbled himself and opened not his mouth; . . . as a sheep that before her shearers is dumb" (Is. 53 : 7). He doubtless sees the essence of the prophecy in the fact that the death of God's Servant is an act of service and that those who are witnesses of it do not know that it is a sacrifice for them.

Jesus is thus convinced that the *meaning* and *effect* of the pre-Messianic tribulation are transferred by God to the suffering and death which he has freely accepted as the future Messiah. His self-sacrifice accordingly has the consequence that the final events have now arrived at the point that they would have reached after

[28] On the suffering Servant of God in Deutero-Isaiah, see p. 16ff.

the tribulation had taken place. This means that the evil world-powers have lost the dominion which they possessed alongside of God's. According to late Jewish eschatology it was their allotted rôle to rise against God in a final contest at the pre-Messianic tribulation, in order that they might suffer destruction at his hands and the Kingdom could then appear. *The death of Jesus thus brings about the coming of the Kingdom of God.* This is its fundamental meaning. The way in which it benefits believers is that it gives them the possibility of entering the Kingdom. At the same time it also benefits them by sparing them the necessity of having to pass through the tribulation before entering the Kingdom.

Jesus' Death is to bring about the Coming of the Kingdom

How can Jesus have arrived at the idea that his death could be of any avail for the bringing about of the Kingdom?

His attitude with regard to the coming of the Kingdom of God is from the very beginning less purely expectant than was usual in late Jewish eschatology. He is, of course, far from regarding believers, as Zarathustra did, as God's comrades in the struggle for the victory of good over evil. Nevertheless he did stand for the view that they could do something to advance the coming of the Kingdom. This can be seen from the words in the speech about the Baptist: "And from the days of John the Baptist until now the Kingdom of heaven suffereth violence, and men of violence take it by force" (Mt. 11 : 12). It has been the fate of this saying to have the most unlikely meanings ascribed to it. The favourite view has been to see in the men of violence people who had misunderstood the Baptist and supposed him to mean that the Kingdom was to be realized by force of arms. But this inevitably gives rise to two questions. How could they possibly have mis-understood the Baptist in this way and, if they had, how could Jesus have let them off so gently? He only mentions them, without any reproach. In reality he has no intention of reproaching them. He is only making it clear that since the preaching of the Baptist men have been exercising pressure on the coming of the Kingdom.

Who are they? Those who believe his message. How do they exercise pressure on the coming of the Kingdom? By the repentance (change of heart) through which they prepare themselves for the coming of the Kingdom. They hope that this will move God to let it appear.

Jesus instructs believers to exercise pressure on the coming of the Kingdom in yet another way. He makes them pray for it in the Lord's Prayer. This prayer is not just a model prayer which he teaches them, but the prayer of entreaty for the coming of the Kingdom. With the first three petitions, Hallowed be thy name, thy Kingdom come, thy will be done in earth as it is in heaven, this is perfectly obvious. With the last two it is equally clear, when we understand them according to their original meaning as an entreaty for the coming of the Kingdom without its being preceded by the pre-Messianic tribulation. And the petition for our daily bread? This, too, as a request for the speedy arrival of the time of the Messianic banquet, is a petition for the coming of the Kingdom of God. As in the last two petitions, so in this too, the literal translation has been ignored because it did not yield any intelligible sense. It is translated, "Give us this day our daily bread", instead of, literally, "Give us to-day, now, our bread for the future". As in the two concluding petitions, so in this, the meaning of the literal translation can be understood only when we take into account the eschatological concept which it presupposes. It is that of the Messianic banquet. In this petition the believers implore God to let the supernatural bread of the expected Messianic banquet appear immediately in place of their ordinary bread.

Jesus' concern with the idea of the Messianic banquet finds expression in the saying that many shall come from east and west and sit down at table with Abraham, Isaac and Jacob in the Kingdom of heaven (Mt. 8 : 11). The two meals which are recorded as miraculous feedings (Mt. 14 : 15–21 and 15 : 32–39) are preliminary celebrations of the Messianic banquet.[29] Jesus lets the crowd which has assembled round him share the provisions

[29] It is possible that Jesus only undertook such a distribution once and that the two accounts refer to the same celebration.

that he and the disciples have brought with them. Each receives a morsel of the food which Jesus has consecrated with a thanksgiving. This means that the recipients, without knowing it, are called to take part in the Messianic banquet. Because they have been table-companions of the Messiah in his concealment and humility, they will be with him also in his glory.

Neither those who took part nor the disciples could grasp the meaning of the meal prepared by Jesus. It has therefore become in the tradition not a celebration but a meal provided to satisfy their hunger, in which a few loaves and fishes were miraculously multiplied so as to become enough for thousands.

The last meal of Jesus with the disciples has the same meaning as these two feedings by the Sea of Galilee. In the course of it he distributes to them bread and wine which have been consecrated by a thanksgiving that he has uttered over them. With the saying about drinking anew of the fruit of the vine with them in his Father's Kingdom he is promising them that they will soon be united with him at the Messianic banquet (Mt. 26 : 26–29).

If Jesus assumed that believers by repentance and entreaty in the Lord's Prayer for the appearance of the Kingdom of God are actually exercising pressure on its coming, this helps to bring everything into focus. We can now understand his conviction that God had ordained that, as the future Messiah, he could by his voluntary suffering and death bring about the coming of the Kingdom without the prior occurrence of the Messianic tribulation. Through his death the two last petitions of the Lord's Prayer find fulfilment.

Does Jesus regard his Death as an Atonement?

Is the only meaning of the death of Jesus that through it the Kingdom is brought about and believers are saved from the necessity of passing through the pre-Messianic tribulation? Is it not at the same time a death of atonement, producing a forgiveness of sins? In the Lord's Prayer the petition for forgiveness and that for protection from the pre-Messianic tribulation come next to each other. It is not clear that there is any connexion between them. The forgiveness of sins for which Jesus bids believers pray in the Lord's Prayer comes from God alone. It presupposes nothing but his compassion and that on their side men have forgiven those who need their forgiveness. This condition must be met in full. It should be noted that the usual translation (the one ordinarily used when the Lord's Prayer is recited in worship) makes it sound milder than it really is. In the text of Matthew it runs not "as we forgive them that trespass against us" but "as we *have forgiven*" (Mt. 6 : 12). What is required is to have forgiven, not just the sentiment of being willing to forgive.

As if this requirement could not be sufficiently impressed upon his hearers, Jesus repeats it after he has dictated the prayer to the believers. "For if ye forgive men their trespasses, your heavenly Father will also forgive you. But if ye forgive not men their trespasses, neither will your Father forgive your trespasses" (Mt. 6 : 14 f.). In the answer to Peter's question, how many times our brother must be forgiven, Jesus tells the parable of the king's servant who deals mercilessly with the fellow-servant who is only slightly in debt to him, whereupon his master, who intended to let him off a large debt, is moved to treat him in the same way (Mt. 18 : 23–35).

In his teaching on the forgiveness of sins Jesus has a forerunner who is seldom mentioned in this connexion, Jesus Sirach. In the collection of proverbs which he made between 190 and 170 B.C. (so some time before the appearance of the Book of Daniel), we read: "He that taketh vengeance shall find vengeance from the Lord; and he will surely make firm his sins. Forgive thy neighbour the hurt that he hath done thee; and then thy sins shall be pardoned when thou prayest. Man cherisheth anger against man; and doth he seek healing from the Lord? Upon a man like himself he hath no mercy; and doth he make supplication for his own sins?" (Ecclus. 28 : 1–4). No saying of Jesus found in the two oldest Gospels would lead to the conclusion that he ever withdrew or expanded the simple teaching in the Lord's Prayer about the forgiveness of sins because of the meaning he attached to his suffering and death.

But is not his death one of atonement in so far as believers are to do penance for their sins in the pre-Messianic tribulation, or in so far as guilt must be cancelled in order that the Kingdom may come at all? This would be a possible assumption in itself. But according to the information we have about the pre-Messianic tribulation from the later prophets and the Apocalypses, the pious have to prove themselves in it, not to expiate sins. Nor is it presupposed in late Jewish eschatology that a load of guilt encumbers the world and is delaying the coming of the Kingdom. In the Apocalypse of Ezra it is expressly stated that the coming of the Kingdom of God, when the time for it has arrived, cannot be delayed by anything, not even by the sins of the dwellers upon earth (4 Ez. 4 : 38–42).[30]

At the Last Supper Jesus says, as he passes round the cup, "This is my blood of the covenant, which is shed for many" (Mk. 14 : 24). He sees his death therefore as a sacrifice offered at the conclusion of the new covenant. In the prophets the Kingdom is regarded as the new covenant which God concludes with his people (Jer. 31 : 31–34; Ezk. 34 : 24 f.). But a sacrifice offered at the conclusion of a covenant is a very different thing from a sacrifice of propitiation. It has nothing to do with the cancelling of sins, but is only an act confirming the compact.

There is, however, mention of propitiatory sacrifice in the passages concerning the suffering Servant in Deutero-Isaiah. His death means that God allows him to bear the guilt of the Gentiles. "But he was wounded for our transgressions, he was bruised for our iniquities: the chastisement of our peace was upon him. . . . The Lord hath laid on him the iniquity of us all" (Is. 53 : 5 f.). Although Jesus applies to himself what is said about the suffering Servant, he does not, so far as we can gather from the two passages in which he alludes to its meaning, regard his death as an atonement, but as an act of service and the payment of a ransom. In accordance with the two last petitions of the Lord's Prayer, he thinks of his sacrifice as an act in consequence of which the pre-Messianic tribulation will not take place. Even if the Servant passages suggest it, Jesus cannot regard his death as a sacrifice

[30] On this passage in 4 Ezra, see p 61.

necessary for the forgiveness of sins. His view of the unconditional forgiveness that comes from God's compassion precludes it.

He sees the essence of the prophecy applying to him in Deutero-Isaiah in the general consideration that the suffering Servant gives his life, unrecognized by those to whose benefit it accrues. The real meaning of his death, however, he finds in its effect in meeting the conditions needed for the coming of the Kingdom. He derives it not from Deutero-Isaiah but from his knowledge of the facts applying to the coming of the Kingdom.[31]

At any rate historical research must reckon with the possibility, with all its far-reaching implications, that, to judge from the indications we have of Jesus' view of the meaning of his death, he did not regard it as an atonement which in any way effected the forgiveness of sins.

Gethsemane

From the time when Jesus disclosed to the disciples the secret that he must suffer and die, there are no more references in his teaching to persecutions which believers must suffer for his sake, and no more warnings not to be offended at him. The pre-Messianic tribulation, together with all that belongs to it, drops out of view. He no longer needs to adjure his own to stand by him and not to doubt him even in his humiliation. In Mk. 8 : 34–38 Jesus tells his disciples and the people that they must not be ashamed of him and his words and must be willing to give their life for him and his gospel. This confirms the view, which is probable on other grounds, that the events recorded in the section Mk. 8 : 34–9 : 29 do not belong to the period after the announce-

---

[31] In the section on the secret of suffering in my *Geschichte der Leben-Jesu-Forschung* (2nd and subsequent editions, pp. 435–437. A shorter and earlier version can be found in *The Quest of the Historical Jesus*, pp. 387–389), I still believed that in the pre-Messianic tribulation a load of guilt that encumbered the world and was delaying the coming of the Kingdom could be expiated by believers, and that Jesus therefore, in accordance with the Servant passages, regarded his vicarious sacrifice as an atonement. As the result of further study of late Jewish eschatology and the thought of Jesus on his passion, I find that I can no longer endorse this view.

ment of his suffering and death, nor to the neighbourhood of Caesarea Philippi, but took place on the shores of the Sea of Galilee, before Jesus withdrew with his disciples to Caesarea Philippi. This was the way in which Jesus had exhorted the disciples in the mission charge, when he was expecting the pre-Messianic tribulation.[32]

Although Jesus is resolved to face suffering and death, he still retains a hope that God may be disposed to dispense with the tribulation without his having to make the sacrifice for which he is ready. There is no limit to the omnipotence of God. In Gethsemane he entreats God three times that this cup may pass him by (Mt. 26 : 37-44). As he had made believers pray in the Lord's Prayer for protection from the tribulation, so he now prays for himself. He takes with him for this prayer James, John and Peter, leaving the other disciples behind. Why are these three to be with him? So that he may have companions to stand by him in his distress? No, the reason is a different one. These three have promised to share with him his death, which is equivalent to the pre-Messianic tribulation. When James and John wanted to sit on his right and left in his glory, and he asked if they were able to drink the cup which he would drink and undergo the baptism in store for him, they answered, "Yes, we are able". He then said to them, "The cup that I drink ye shall drink; and with the baptism that I am baptized withal shall ye be baptized" (Mk. 10 : 35-39). This shows that it was his conviction that they were destined to suffer and die with him. He assumes the same of Peter since, on the way to Gethsemane, when he foretold that he would deny him three times, Peter replied, "Even if I must die with thee, yet will I not deny thee" (Mt. 26 : 33-35).

Now that the time has come, he is anxious for these three that they may really be about to suffer and die with him. That is why they are to be with him and watch with him now. His entreaty includes them too. If God grants him not to have to drink the cup, they will escape too. When they let themselves be overcome by sleep, he warns them, "Watch and pray, that

[32] On the question whether the events reported in the section Mk. 8 : 34–9 : 29 did not occur earlier by the Sea of Galilee, see p 111.

ye enter not into temptation: the spirit indeed is willing, but the flesh is weak" (Mt. 26 : 41). Here it is plain from the whole situation that the *peirasmos* (πειρασμός) cannot mean any temptation to give way to evil, but only a testing in suffering and the agony of death, corresponding to the pre-Messianic tribulation. The text (ἵνα μὴ εἰσέλθητε εἰς πειρασμόν) speaks clearly of "entering into" the testing. It must not therefore be translated "that you do not fall into temptation". The peculiar testing (*peirasmos*) into which God "leads" the believers according to the penultimate petition of the Lord's Prayer, and which the three disciples in Gethsemane are in danger of "entering", is the pre-Messianic tribulation, or a form of testing through suffering and the agony of death which corresponds to it. Only when this is borne in mind can the text in these two passages be allowed to read as it does.

The three were spared the suffering and death with Jesus which they had presumed to accept. He need not have been anxious for them. He alone goes to his death.

CHAPTER III

PRIMITIVE CHRISTIAN BELIEF
IN THE KINGDOM OF GOD

I. THE RESURRECTION OF JESUS AND THE COMING
OF THE KINGDOM OF GOD

Belief in the Resurrection and in the Messiahship of Jesus

In what does the primitive Christian faith consist? The fundamental element in it is belief in the immediate coming of the
Kingdom of God, as it has been preached by John the Baptist and
Jesus. To this article of faith which was already present, now,
after his death, another is added; belief in his Messiahship. The
believers know through the disciples and from Jesus' acknowledgement before the High Priest that he regarded himself as the coming
Messiah. Because of their belief in his resurrection they are
convinced that this is what he is. To primitive Christian belief,
and it is important to take this into account, Jesus was not the
Messiah during his earthly existence. He became it only in the
supernatural state that he acquired through the resurrection. The
view that it was as a man who had become the Messiah that he
walked on earth and preached arises only in a later generation,
no longer familiar with the eschatological outlook belonging to
Jesus and primitive Christianity.

The earliest Christian believers are convinced of the bodily
resurrection of Jesus. It has been established through visions in
which he was seen by several of them. The earliest tradition does
not know of any appearances of Jesus from which the material
reality of his bodily presence could be inferred. Stories of this kind
arise only in later traditions. This later tradition is found in Luke
and the Fourth Gospel. In Lk. 24 : 36–43 Jesus bids the disciples
touch his feet and eats a piece of broiled fish before their eyes.
In John 20 : 26–29 he lets Thomas put his hands in the scar made
by the spear-thrust.

The visionary nature of the appearance of Jesus is attested by

Paul in the account he gives in 1 Corinthians: "He appeared to Cephas; then to the twelve; then he appeared to above five hundred brethren at once, of whom the greater part remain until now, but some are fallen asleep; then he appeared to James; then to all the apostles; and last of all. . . . he appeared to me also" (1 Cor. 15 : 5–8). Peter, who saw Jesus illuminated with heavenly radiance together with Moses and Elijah on the Mount of Transfiguration (Mk. 9 : 2–8), was also the first to have a vision of the risen Lord.

This ecstatic experience depends upon the fact that Jesus, when he informed his disciples that he would have to die in Jerusalem, promised them at the same time that he would soon rise again. There has been a disposition to assume that the earliest tradition made Jesus promise his resurrection because belief in the resurrection had arisen in the primitive church. In point of fact the position is that this belief arose in consequence of Jesus' promise of his resurrection. To understand the visionary experience of Peter we must take into consideration the fact that the women who had come to the tomb in which he had been laid early in the morning on the third day, in order to embalm the body, found the tomb empty. When and by whom he had been removed from it will never be established.

The Appearances of the Risen Lord in Jerusalem and Galilee

How does Jesus picture his resurrection and manifestation in Messianic glory? Did he expect to be transformed into the Son of Man immediately at the resurrection and as such to appear on the clouds of heaven, or did he assume that this would happen later, as a separate event?

When he held out to the disciples on sending them out on their mission the prospect that the appearance of the Son of Man would take place before they had finished visiting the cities of Israel (Mt. 10 : 23), he doubtless supposed that during the pre-Messianic tribulation he would immediately be transformed into the Son of Man, whether as one who had survived it or as one who had suffered death in it. Does he also expect on the night before his death, when he presents the prospect of his appearance on the clouds of heaven as Son of Man to the High Priest and his judges, that this will happen immediately at the resurrection? We have one saying of his which makes this unlikely. On the way to Gethsemane he says to his disciples, "But after I am raised up, I will go before you into Galilee" (Mt. 26 : 32). The most natural interpretation of this saying is that he thinks that after he has risen he will proceed to Galilee at the head of his disciples, as he came at their head from Galilee to suffer in Jerusalem (Mk. 10 : 32).[1]

It can hardly be supposed that Jesus thought that he would march in procession before the disciples as Son of Man. The Son of Man does not walk on earth, but proceeds on the clouds of heaven. After he has risen from the dead Jesus intends to go with the disciples to Galilee because it is there, where he had come forward proclaiming the coming of the Kingdom and had gathered the believers around him, that he expects to be revealed in his Messianic glory. Jerusalem, the city which kills and stones those who are sent to it by God, and upon which he has pronounced sentence at the end of his speech to the Pharisees (Mt. 23 : 37–39), is never considered in this connexion.

Because of the words spoken on the way to Gethsemane, the disciples, and with them a hundred and twenty believers from Galilee (Acts 1 : 14 f., 2 : 7), stay on after the death of Jesus in Jerusalem. Here they experience appearances of the risen Lord. But still he does not lead them to Galilee. This promise is not fulfilled. It is testimony to the reliability of the accounts in Matthew and Mark that the saying about going before them into Galilee was nevertheless preserved. Later tradition seeks to find a fulfilment of this unfulfilled promise. In the concluding section of Matthew which forms part of this tradition the angels (Mt. 28 : 7) and the risen Lord himself (Mt. 28 : 10) charge the women at the empty tomb to inform the disciples that they are to go to Galilee in order to see him there. According to

---

[1] There is a close correspondence between the words, "And they were in the way, going up to Jerusalem; and Jesus was going before them" (Mk. 10 : 32), and the other saying, "I will go before you into Galilee" (Mk. 14 : 28).

Mt. 28 : 16–20 they are then with him on a mountain there and receive from him the commission to preach the gospel throughout the whole world and to baptize. This later tradition misunderstands the saying of Jesus on the way to Gethsemane. It takes "going before them" as meaning that the risen Lord will go to Galilee and there await the disciples. In reality, of course, Jesus is thinking of taking the lead in a common journey to Galilee. This is how the disciples actually understood it. They remain in Jerusalem in the expectation of going to Galilee with the risen master who has already appeared to Peter. A still later tradition has it that they remained in Jerusalem because the risen Lord bade them wait there to receive the Holy Spirit (Lk. 24 : 49, Acts 1 : 8).

The oldest conception of the risen Lord was probably that he was dwelling on earth and from here appearing to his own. This corresponds to the saying of Jesus that when he was risen he would go with the disciples to Galilee. According to Acts resurrection appearances took place during a period of forty days (Acts 1 : 1–3). After the cessation of the appearances the view arose that the risen Lord was now in heaven and would descend from there to earth in his Messianic glory. In the vision which he has before his stoning Stephen sees the heaven open and the Son of Man standing at the right hand of God (Acts 7 : 55). Paul, on the road to Damascus, hears the voice of Jesus from heaven (Acts 9 : 3–6). In the Epistle to the Philippians he writes: "For our citizenship is in heaven; from whence also we wait for a Saviour, the Lord Jesus Christ" (Phil. 3 : 20). In accordance with this changed conception of the abode of the risen Lord, the later tradition records that after his sojourn on earth he took leave of his disciples and ascended to heaven (Lk. 24 : 50 f., Acts 1 : 9–11).

Strictly speaking we should speak of Jesus' coming as Messiah, not of his return. For the earliest Christian believers his appearance in glory as the Messiah, expected in the immediate future, was so much in the foreground of their faith that they use for it the term Parousia ($\pi\alpha\varrho o\upsilon\sigma\acute{\iota}\alpha$), arrival. His previous human existence is not included in it. We find it more natural to speak of his return, and there is no reason why we should give up doing so.

We must only bear in mind that for believers of the earliest period it was not the Jesus who had come forward in Galilee, but only the risen Lord, who was the Messiah.

The Atoning Death of Jesus and the Forgiveness of Sins

There arose in primitive Christianity another belief beside that in the Messiahship of Jesus. This was the belief that through his death the forgiveness of sins was available for believers. How did it arise?

Jesus did not consider it necessary to explain the meaning of his death to his followers. They did not need to know it nor to believe in it. At the appearance of the Kingdom, which he expected immediately, they would experience the way in which his passion was of benefit to them. When, however, the Kingdom did not come at once, but continued to be the object of expectation, believers found themselves in the position of having to form some conception of the meaning of his death. They could not find it in the two vague and obscure allusions to his death as a ransom for many (Mk. 10 : 45) and his blood as the blood of the covenant shed for them. Moreover, they felt delivered from any such necessity. Jesus had pointed to the fact that his death could be studied in the scriptures. "The Son of Man goeth, even as it is written of him" (Mt. 26 : 24). "Thinkest thou that I cannot beseech my Father, and he shall even now send me more than twelve legions of angels? How then should the scriptures be fulfilled, that thus it must be?" (Mt. 26 : 53 f.). On the meaning of his death, the only passage that comes under consideration for believers is Isaiah 53.[2] Here it is written that he has borne the sufferings of many in order to help the people to attain righteousness. The death of the suffering Servant is an atoning death. Moreover, believers were firmly convinced that in consequence of the death of Jesus they did participate in the forgiveness of sins which was a necessary condition of entry into the Kingdom.

Jesus himself finds it foretold in Isaiah 53 that he must take upon

[2] For the original meaning of this section, see p. 17f.; on the meaning that it had for Jesus, see p. 121ff.

himself a death that serves others. But he does not derive the meaning of his death from the conception of atoning death found in this passage. The forgiveness of sins is no problem to him. He stands by the view which he has laid down in the Lord's Prayer. The meaning of the sacrifice demanded of him reveals itself to him as an outcome of the problem of the coming of the Kingdom. The problem lies in the delay in the appearance of the pre-Messianic tribulation and of his manifestation as Son of Man, which he had expected at once when he sent out the disciples on their mission (Mt. 10). He goes to his death in order to fulfil in himself the pre-Messianic tribulation and so bring about the coming of the Kingdom which was to follow upon it.[3]

The first believers accepted without question the idea that by his death Jesus was imparting to them the forgiveness necessary for entry into the Kingdom. They did so because the Baptist had granted those who were awaiting the Kingdom with him just such a forgiveness of sins through his baptism. Naturally the believers who were with Jesus expected to receive the same from him. In applying Isaiah 53 to him they were led to see his death as an atoning death which provided them with forgiveness of their sins.

The idea of a forgiveness of sins to be obtained in a special way with a view to entering the Kingdom of God originates therefore with the Baptist. Combined with Isaiah 53 it forms the presupposition for the rise of the view of the death of Jesus which sees it as an atonement. Paul writes to the Corinthians: "I delivered unto you first of all that which also I received, how that Christ died for our sins according to the scriptures . . ." (1 Cor. 15 : 3). Because they had at their disposal no clear saying of Jesus about the meaning of his death, the first believers concluded from Isaiah 53 that by his death he had secured for them the forgiveness of sins that would enable them to enter the Kingdom. And this means that from the beginning there were two doctrines of forgiveness existing side by side in Christianity. That contained in the Lord's Prayer is simple. That which is based on the conception of the atoning death of Jesus involves

[3] See p. 123f.

questions and difficulties that no explanation can settle. How could God conceivably need the sacrificial death of Jesus in order to forgive sins? If knowledge of the atoning death of Jesus and faith in it are really necessary for the forgiveness of sins, how are we to understand that in the Old Testament God forgives sins without any further requirement, purely out of compassion, and Jesus presupposes such forgiveness? How on that view can those who die without having heard of Jesus obtain forgiveness of their sins?

The reason for all the difficulties of the view of the forgiveness of sins built on the conception of the atoning death of Jesus lies in this. Something timeless, God's forgiveness, and something which took place in time, the death of Jesus, are being combined in such a way that the timeless factor is to be made dependent on that which belongs to time.

The emergence of the view of forgiveness based on the conception of the atoning death of Jesus has from the first had a further consequence. This is that the condition for obtaining the forgiveness of sins put forward by Jesus in the Lord's Prayer and the words which follow it as being the sole, but absolutely indispensable, requirement loses its rightful significance. The strict demand that we must prepare ourselves for the obtaining of forgiveness by a complete forgiving of others at once ceases to dominate the whole view of forgiveness. Here, too, the ethical element in the religion of Jesus has not been completely taken over into that of Christians. It has had to accommodate itself for centuries to taking a back place behind dogmatic statements about forgiveness. The simple and powerful ethical teaching of Jesus about the forgiveness of sins has been overshadowed by the doctrine of his atoning death.

The Bestowal of the Holy Spirit as a Sign of the Nearness of the Kingdom

Alongside of belief in the Messiahship of Jesus and belief in the forgiveness of sins in consequence of his atoning death there appears also the belief that the bestowal of the Spirit has actually taken place.

While the first believers and the apostles were assembled at the Jewish harvest festival celebrated fifty days after the Passover, something happened to them which they regarded as the fulfilment of the prophecy of Joel (Joel 2 : 28 f.) about the outpouring of the Spirit of God on all flesh.[4] They fell into a state of trance in which they "spoke with tongues". Glossolaly, speaking with tongues, consists in speaking in a state of intense ecstatic excitement in sounds which do not belong to ordinary modes of utterance. This was understood by the early Christians as speech in a supernatural, Spirit-given language. Such ecstatic speech was a common occurrence in primitive Christianity. The peculiarity of this occasion is that they communicated it to others and enabled them to start speaking with tongues.

Paul discusses speaking with tongues in 1 Corinthians (1 Cor. 14 : 1–28). He sees it as a gift imparted by God and conceives of it as speaking and praying in the Spirit. The hearers cannot understand this monologue of the Spirit. Paul therefore insists that those who have the gift of interpreting this ecstatic speech should be at pains to reproduce what is said in it in ordinary language. He states decisively that speaking with tongues occupies too great a place in worship. Although he can boast of having this gift in a high degree himself, he prefers to instruct and edify believers in ordinary speech. Little by little speaking with tongues ceased to play a part in early Christianity. In later times it has reappeared from time to time in enthusiastic movements within Christianity. Even modern church history, especially the history of missions, occasionally reports instances of it.

In Acts (Acts 2 : 1–13) the first speaking with tongues in Jerusalem at Pentecost is misunderstood and taken to mean that they spoke in foreign languages, so that pilgrims who had come to the feast from Cappadocia, Pontus, Asia, Phrygia, Pamphylia, Egypt, Libya, Italy, Crete and Arabia shared with one another the miracle of hearing people from Galilee preach "the mighty works of God" in all these languages. This building up of the event into a miracle belongs to a later tradition.

Speaking with tongues is the proof to Paul, as it had been to the

[4] On this prophecy of Joel, see p. 22.

Apostles and the first believers, that the coming of the Spirit has taken place.

2. BAPTISM AND COMMUNION

Baptism in Primitive Christianity

Everything which constitutes primitive Christian belief is brought into relation with baptism. In that it was administered in the name of Jesus, it means acceptance into the fellowship of those who believe in the Messiahship of Jesus and await the speedy appearance of the Kingdom of God, certain that they will participate in it. Through baptism the believer obtains the forgiveness of sins which will enable him to enter the Kingdom and which has been made available by the atoning death of Jesus. Through it he obtains the capacity to receive the Spirit. Primitive Christianity takes over the baptism of John and turns it into Christian baptism. How does this come about?

Strictly speaking, the baptism of John cannot be repeated. In virtue of the authority accorded him he bestows by his baptism the forgiveness of sins. After his death no one can impart it any longer. There are still disciples of John, but there is no longer the baptism of John. In the Temple at Jerusalem Jesus speaks of it as something belonging to the past. He asks the scribes, "The baptism of John, was it from heaven, or from men?" (Mk. 11 : 30). Jesus does not baptize and in the oldest tradition does not give any sort of commission to baptize. The account at the end of the Gospel of Matthew (Mt. 28 : 16–20) belongs to a tradition that arose at a later date. It arose because it seemed by that time incredible that baptism should have arisen without instructions from Jesus. That this tradition does not come from the earliest period is plain from the fact that Jesus orders baptism in the name of Father, Son and Spirit, a formula which came into use only at the end of the first century. In primitive Christianity it was in the name of Jesus.[5]

In the view of Jesus the believers who have gathered round him

[5] See p. 141.

in expectation of the Kingdom of God have no need of baptism
to survive the Judgement and enter the Kingdom. Without
knowing it, they are in this world companions of the future
Messiah who will conduct the Judgement and bring in the
Kingdom. This guarantees for them that they will be with him
in the world to come. For Jesus, therefore, there cannot be any
question of baptism. Belonging to him effects and guarantees
salvation. The authority of the future Messiah is far greater than
that of the Baptist. It continues to operate without any question in
those who come into relation with him.

He never considers the possibility that after his death a sacramental practice corresponding to the baptism of John might
become necessary to procure the forgiveness of sins for new
believers. He does not reckon with new believers, but only with
those around him. He expects the immediate appearance of the
Kingdom and not the rise of an ever-growing community
believing in him as the Messiah.

That, however, is what occurred. A practice by which new
adherents could be received into the existing fellowship became
essential. The baptism once practised by John for the forgiveness
of sins presented itself as the solution. It was taken over and
Christianized. It should be noted that at the first baptism on the
feast of Pentecost only new believers were baptized, not the
apostles and the hundred and twenty believers from Galilee who
were with them, although neither the apostles nor these had ever
been baptized. As men who had been with Jesus they did not need
baptism. The new believers were baptized by these unbaptized
Christians. Paul, though he is called to be an apostle in a vision
of the risen Lord which is vouchsafed to him, still needs baptism.

The adoption of John's baptism was made all the easier by the
fact that the growth in the congregation of believers in the
Messiah took place in Judaea, the home of the Baptist's followers.
It was also facilitated by the fact that the memory of his baptism
was still quite fresh. He was beheaded only a few months before
the crucifixion of Jesus. It was important too that Jesus, in a
speech given before his believers in Galilee, had ascribed a unique
importance to the Baptist (Mt. 11 : 7–15) and had given the

Pharisees and scribes to understand in the Temple at Jerusalem that he regarded the baptism of John as something that came from God (Mk. 11 : 27-33).[6]

The difficulty that there could be no real repetition of baptism as an act practised by John with his personal authority was removed by the fact that it now took place in the name of Jesus. He who administers this baptism no longer needs any special authority. The person baptized in the name of Jesus thereby enters into a special relation with him, the future Messiah, which constitutes its efficacy. The forgiveness of sins which comes through it is won through him. The baptized now receive from him what had earlier been obtained through the authority of John. Because forgiveness of sins through Jesus replaces that obtained through John, Christian baptism is the continuation of his and corresponds to it.

Since this baptism leads to the reception of the Holy Spirit, it is the fulfilment of the prophecy of the Baptist about the greater than he who would come after him and baptize with the Holy Spirit (Mk. 1 : 7 f.). According to this saying he expected that those who had received the forgiveness of sins through baptism with water would subsequently receive the Holy Spirit through the one who was greater than he.[7]

In Acts we read of baptism by John and Christian baptism existing side by side. We are told that there were twelve Christians in Ephesus who had only received the baptism of John and knew only of this, not of the baptism which conferred the Spirit. When baptized by Paul in the name of Jesus they partake of the Spirit through the laying on of his hands (Acts 19 : 1-7).

For the earliest period the theory that the reception of the Spirit presupposes baptism with water cannot be wholly maintained. The apostles and the hundred and twenty believers from Galilee who are with them in Jerusalem receive it without having been baptized. It is not unknown for believers to fall into ecstasy and speak with tongues before they have received baptism. This

---

[6] On the attitude of Jesus to the Baptist, see p. 75f.

[7] On the Baptist's view of the greater one who was to come after him, see p. 78f.

happens with Cornelius and his household while Peter is preaching the gospel to him. Because this has befallen them, they are at once baptized without further question (Acts 10 : 44–48).[8]

The view that at baptism in the name of Jesus the forgiveness of sins and the capacity to receive the gift of the Spirit both go together must have been present in Christianity from the beginning. Paul presupposes it and argues from it. "For in *one* Spirit were we all baptized into *one* body . . .; and were all made to drink of *one* Spirit" (1 Cor. 12 : 13). In Acts Peter expounds the meaning of baptism in his speech at Pentecost in the words, "Repent ye, and be baptized every one of you in the name of Jesus Christ unto the remission of your sins; and ye shall receive the gift of the Holy Ghost" (Acts 2 : 38). Through the sheer logic of events, without any relevant command of Jesus, the baptism with water practised by John was taken over into Christianity and Christianized.

The Christianized form had this in common with the baptism of John (and it is important to note this) that it bestowed forgiveness only for sins already committed. Neither by John nor in primitive Christian doctrine is there any suggestion of forgiveness for those which the believer commits subsequently. That the forgiveness of sins is limited in this way is to be explained by the intensity of eschatological expectation. It is assumed by primitive Christianity, as it was by John the Baptist, that by making the proper effort the believer can remain in the condition of sanctity which baptism has conferred upon him during the days remaining until the appearance of the Kingdom. But as time went on the days and weeks passed into months and years. Faith had to come to terms with the fact that the baptized would probably not experience the coming of the Kingdom, but would have to pass their whole existence after baptism still in the corporal state, with its inclination to sin. This meant that the forgiveness of sins received at baptism was not enough. The possibility of sins

[8] An extraordinary requirement appears in the account in Acts according to which the Samaritans who have been baptized by Philip in the name of Jesus have to wait to receive the Spirit until Peter and James come from Jerusalem and lay their hands upon them (Acts 8 : 5–17).

committed after baptism became a problem with which Christian doctrine had to wrestle for centuries, without finding any satisfactory solution.

The writer of the so-called First Epistle of Peter deals with the difficulty arising from the primitive Christian view that forgiveness of sins can be obtained only through faith in the atoning death of Jesus and baptism. He is looking for an answer to the question how the generations which lived before the appearance of Jesus can partake of the forgiveness of sins without having met the necessary conditions. He finds the answer in the assumption that Jesus preached the gospel to the spirits of the dead in the under-world between his death and resurrection (1 Pet. 3 : 19 f., 4; 6). In a work written in Rome, c. 140, and circulating under the title of "The Shepherd of Hermas" (*Pastor Hermae*), the view is advanced that those who died before the time of Christ must undergo baptism at the resurrection in order to enter into blessedness.

The Communion

It is the same with the repetition of the last meal of Jesus with his disciples as with the baptism of John: it is of great significance in primitive Christianity without having been commanded by Jesus and although it would appear to be incapable of repetition. The accounts of the Last Supper in Matthew and Mark do not contain a word ordering its repetition. Since, however, it was later repeated it seemed self-evident that this must be by his direction. A saying to this effect therefore came to be accepted in the account of the last meal with the disciples. It had already happened before the time of Paul. The words of Jesus at the Last Supper, as he quotes them to the Corinthians in the course of his directions for its celebration, include the command to repeat it. "For I received of the Lord that which also I delivered unto you, how that the Lord Jesus in the night in which he was betrayed took bread; and when he had given thanks, he brake it, and said, This is my body, which is for you: this do in remembrance of me. In like manner also the cup, after supper, saying, This cup is the new covenant in my blood: this do, as oft as ye drink it, in remembrance of me" (1 Cor. 11 : 23–25).

This is probably the first instance in which it can be proved with such certainty that the tradition has been influenced by an idea which only arose in primitive Christianity. Once again, moreover, the reliability of the account in Matthew and Mark comes out. It is astonishing that the words of Jesus at the Last Supper were preserved by them in their original form when the temptation to insert in them the command to repeat it was so strong that even Paul succumbed to it. Strangely enough, in Luke the words spoken at the Last Supper include the command to repeat it only with the breaking of the bread (Lk. 22 : 16–20). It is also worth noting that in Paul and Luke it is no longer "shed for many" as in Matthew and Mark, but "shed for you". By this alteration the saying of Jesus acquires a setting in which it applies to those who are present at the celebration at any time.

In his famous *Christian Faith*, published in 1821, Friedrich Schleiermacher (1768–1834) for the first time dared to suggest that the repetition of the last meal of Jesus with his disciples had arisen in primitive Christianity without any instruction from him. In Schleiermacher's opinion the disciples had introduced this practice on their own.

How did this come about? Why did they consider this celebration a practice required by the faith? How far was the original celebration, at which Jesus was present, speaking and acting, capable of being repeated at all? Schleiermacher does not deal with this question.

If we are to begin to understand the almost incredible fact that the celebration was repeated, we must start by establishing what the real nature of the celebration that was repeated was. In the earliest period, according to Acts, it was called "the breaking of bread". In Paul it is called "the Lord's Supper". "And they continued stedfastly in the apostles' teaching and fellowship, and in the breaking of bread and the prayers" (Acts 2 : 42). "And day by day, continuing stedfastly with one accord in the temple, and breaking bread at home, they did take their food with gladness and singleness of heart, praising God" (Acts 2 : 46 f.).

We gain valuable information about the celebration from the way in which Paul remonstrates with the Corinthians over the manner in which they usually conducted it. "When therefore ye assemble yourselves together, it is not possible to eat the Lord's supper [properly]: for in your eating each one taketh before other his own supper; and one is hungry, and another is drunken. What? Have ye not houses [of your own] to eat and to drink in? Or despise ye the Church of God, and put them to shame that have not? . . . Shall I praise you in this? I praise you not" (1 Cor. 11 : 20-22). "Wherefore, my brethren, when ye come together to eat [in communion], wait for one another. If any man is hungry, let him eat at home [beforehand]" (1 Cor. 11 : 33 f.). The very remarkable fact emerges from this account that this primitive Christian celebration was a community meal at which there was thanksgiving and exultation (Acts 2 : 47). Although it is a repetition of the last meal of Jesus with his disciples, it is not a funeral meal, but a festive one.

In the period following Paul it is described as ἀγάπη (love feast) and εὐχαριστία (thanksgiving meal). As time goes on the latter becomes generally established as the most appropriate designation. Not only bread, but any kind of food can be used at the Eucharist. It is a genuine common meal, to which each believer brings his own contribution.

Jesus' words about the bread and wine being his body and blood, incredible as it seems, play no part in this meal. They are never mentioned. Paul quotes them (1 Cor. 11 : 23-26), in order to help the Corinthians to understand that the meal is not only a festive one, but also a commemoration of Jesus' death, which ought not therefore to degenerate into an orgy. The way in which he alludes to the words makes it clear that they are not familiar to the Corinthians as part of the celebration. Nor does he insist that they should immediately make use of them at it. He does not think of expounding them in the sense that the forgiveness of sins earned by the atoning death of Jesus is obtained in the eating and drinking of the elements.

The words of Jesus about the bread and wine as being his flesh and blood, which we regard as the essence of the Last Supper, did

not constitute its main significance for the disciples and the first
believers. They found it rather in the thanksgiving over the
bread and wine uttered at an earlier point. The words about
bread and wine as his body and blood are only two similitudes
with reference to his approaching death which he adds to the
thanksgiving. For the disciples the meal is one of thanksgiving.
It is as such that they repeat it. As such it is repeatable. The thanksgiving, which is modelled on that which Jesus gave at the Last
Supper, can be spoken by others.

But what is the thanksgiving for? Not only for food and drink,
as they lie ready to be enjoyed. The grace involved is of a special
and higher kind. In it thanks are given to God for the Messianic
banquet to which the believers are looking forward at this
gathering to a communal meal with one another, and for the
Kingdom which will shortly appear.

At the thanksgiving meal which Jesus celebrated with his
disciples it is clear that there is a connexion for him and his
disciples with the Messianic banquet. This finds expression in his
words as he passes round the cup. He reveals to them that he will
not drink again of the fruit of the vine until the day when he
drinks it with them anew in his Father's Kingdom (Mt. 26 : 29).
The significance which the expectation of the Messianic banquet
has for him comes out also in the fact that in the Lord's Prayer
he makes the faithful entreat God that he may let them partake
of the future bread (the Messianic banquet) immediately
(Mt. 6 : 11).[9] He had already held a thanksgiving meal with the
believers in Galilee and made them share some of the food over
which he had pronounced a thanksgiving. In this way, without
knowing it, they became table-companions of the future Messiah,
and thereby secured an invitation to be his companions also at
the Messianic banquet.[10]

Since the words in which Jesus pronounced thanksgiving at the
celebration by the Sea of Galilee and at the Last Supper with the
disciples are not recorded in the tradition, it might be supposed
that it was a simple expression of thanks for food and drink. In

[9] On this, see p. 124.
[10] On the thanksgiving meal with the believers in Galilee, see p. 124f.

Acts, however, we are told of thanksgiving with jubilation and exultation at the breaking of bread (Acts 2 : 46 f.), and we know from Paul that those who had spiritual gifts burst out into speaking with tongues in their thanksgiving (1 Cor. 14 : 14–17). This makes it probable that there was something special about this thanksgiving.

The oldest eucharistic prayers that we have provide confirmation that the thanksgiving referred to the Messianic banquet and the coming of the Kingdom of God. They are found in an early Christian writing which bears the title "Teaching of the Twelve Apostles" and is generally quoted under the name of *Didache* (teaching). Only the title was known until in the year 1873 the text was discovered by the Metropolitan of Nicomedia, Philotheos Bryennios, in a manuscript of the year 1056 in the Jerusalem monastery at Constantinople, and published in 1883. Through this work we have a knowledge of Christianity in the form in which it existed in Palestine towards the end of the first century.

Here are some excerpts from the eucharistic prayers in the *Didache*. Before the meal: "We give thee thanks, O our Father, for the life and knowledge which thou didst make known to us through Jesus, thy son. To thee be glory for ever. As this broken bread was scattered upon the mountains, and, being gathered together, became one, so may thy church be gathered together from the ends of the earth into thy Kingdom. For thine is the glory and the power through Jesus Christ for ever" (Did. 9 : 3 f.). After the meal: "Thou, Almighty Ruler, didst create all things for thy name's sake, and didst give food and drink to men for enjoyment, that they might render thanks to thee; but didst bestow upon us spiritual food and drink and eternal life through thy Servant. Above all we give thee thanks that thou art mighty. To thee be glory for ever. Remember, Lord, thy church, to deliver it from all evil and to perfect it in thy love, and gather it together from the four winds, the sanctified church, into thy Kingdom. For thine is the power and the glory for ever. May grace come and may this world pass away. Hosanna to the God of David. If any man is holy, let him come; if any man is not, let him repent. Marana tha. Amen" (Did. 10 : 3–6).

Thus petition is made in this thanksgiving that this world may pass away, the Kingdom come, and Jesus appear in glory as Messiah. This is the reference in the Aramaic invocation Marana tha (תא מלנא, Our Lord, come!). That this cry which concludes the celebration is in Aramaic, while the prayers are handed down in Greek, shows that it originated in the earliest period, when the prayers were spoken in Aramaic.

Marana tha comes also in Paul, in the conclusion of 1 Corinthians written in his own hand. "If any man loveth not the Lord, let him be anathema. Marana tha" (1 Cor. 16 : 22). This sentence gives the impression of coming from a prayer at the celebration of the Lord's Supper. In a Greek translation ('Αμήν, ἔρχου, κύριε 'Ιησοῦ, Amen: come, Lord Jesus) Marana tha concludes the Apocalypse of John (Rev. 22 : 20).

The thanksgiving meal in expectation of the coming of the Kingdom is the only service of worship in the earliest period. Purely preaching services are unknown at this time. All prayer, prophecy and teaching take place during the celebration of the meal. Paul is the first to make an effort to create a place for instruction and edification in the thanksgiving service. As time went on the reading of accounts of the preaching of Jesus and of apostolic writings came into use during the celebration.

Eucharist and Expectation of the Parousia

The saying of Jesus about drinking wine anew with the disciples in his Father's Kingdom took on for them the meaning of a command to repeat the celebration. Their interpretation of it was that during a thanksgiving meal he would come to them to celebrate it with them as a Messianic banquet in the Kingdom which would appear at the moment of this return. Day after day, probably from the first Easter on, they and the hundred and twenty believers from Galilee kept on celebrating the thanksgiving meal in order that the hope aroused by that saying might come to fulfilment. They held the daily thanksgiving meal in the same room in which they were with Jesus at the Last Supper and heard from his lips the promise of their reunion at the drinking of the wine anew.

It may be inferred from the account in Acts that the disciples and the believers from Galilee met in the house of the mother of John Mark, who later accompanied Barnabas and Paul on the First Missionary Journey (Acts 12 : 25). It was in this house that Peter found them assembled on his escape from prison (Acts 12 : 12–17). The meeting-place of the believers is the upper room (ὑπερῷον), which means a room situated immediately under the flat roof (Acts 1 : 12–14). It must have been a large one, to hold the entire company. It was in this room that the believers were "all together in one place" on the day of Pentecost (Acts 2 : 1). How did it come to be identical with the room in which Jesus celebrated the Last Supper with the disciples?

When Jesus sent two disciples (from Bethany) to the city with instructions to prepare the Passover meal for him, he told them that they were to follow a man who would meet them with a pitcher of water. He would lead them to a house with a *large* upper room furnished with rugs (ἀνάγαιον μέγα ἐστρωμένον. Ἀνάγαιον is synonymous with ὑπερῷον), where they were then to prepare the meal. We owe this valuable piece of information to the Gospel of Mark (Mk. 14 : 13–15), which rests on a tradition going back to John Mark. Matthew only relates that Jesus sent the two disciples with directions to inform someone in the city, "The Master saith, My time is at hand; I keep the Passover at thy house with my disciples" (Mt. 26 : 18). Theodor Zahn was one of the first to put forward the view that the house of the last meal of Jesus with his disciples was identical with that of John Mark's mother, in which the disciples met together with the believers from Galilee in the period immediately following the death of Jesus.[11]

Stories of the resurrection appearances belonging to the later tradition allow the expectation of the disciples that Jesus would again celebrate the meal with them to find fulfilment. When the

[11] Theodor Zahn, *Einleitung in das Neue Testament*, 2nd ed. 1900, Vol. II, pp. 213, 242–245, 252. E.T. (ed. Jacobus), 2nd ed. New York 1917, Vol. II, pp. 447 f., 490–494, 505.

risen Lord eats and drinks in these stories with his own, or in their vicinity, it is not only the reality of his bodily presence that is demonstrated. The conviction that at his reappearance a meal would take place has an importance of its own.

A later tradition of this kind underlies the words of Peter in the house of Cornelius, that Jesus, after his resurrection, ate and drank with the disciples (Acts 10 : 40 f.). So too when in Luke (Lk. 24 : 13–31) the risen Lord breaks bread with the two disciples at Emmaus, and again when in the Fourth Gospel (Jn. 21 : 1–14) the disciples get out of the boat on the Sea of Galilee and he is waiting for them with a meal prepared on the shore and distributes to them bread and fish. Justin Martyr (100–165), in his Dialogue with Trypho the Jew, written about 150, quotes as an important piece of the preaching of Jesus that he will come again to Jerusalem and then eat and drink anew with his disciples (Dial. Try. 51 : 2).

Although the thanksgiving meal of the first Christians goes back to that which Jesus celebrated with the disciples, it did not take place in the evening but in the morning. This was necessary because the return of Jesus was expected to take place at it. In view of the belief that his resurrection had occurred in the morning, it was assumed that his return would take place at this time of day. It is therefore inaccurate to speak of a celebration of the Lord's Supper in the early church. It knew of no supper, but only of the eucharist, the morning thanksgiving meal which had grown out of that evening one.

It is this fact that in the earliest period of all the appearance of Jesus at the meal was hoped and prayed for which explains the enthusiastic nature of the celebration. It is highly probable that the speaking with tongues on the morning of Pentecost began during the prayers at the thanksgiving meal. The simplest explanation of the gathering of the believers on that morning would be to suppose that they had come together for the celebration. The state of excitement of the participants, and particularly of the speakers of the thanksgiving prayers, provided the conditions for the manifestation of the ecstasy.

After Pentecost large numbers of new believers were added to the one hundred and twenty of the first weeks, and the thanksgiving meal was no longer celebrated in the upper room of the house of John Mark's mother alone, but also in several different assemblies meeting in different places. This meant that it was no longer possible to believe that Jesus would appear at a meal celebrated by the disciples together with the believers from Galilee in the room in which the Last Supper had taken place. This view was replaced by the more general idea, looking to a celebration held in several places at the same time, that the return of Jesus would take place simultaneously with the celebration.

This, however, presupposes that the many celebrations are all being held on the same day at the same hour. This usage began to develop quite early and of its own accord, since the daily celebration became impossible for practical reasons. In the course of time the celebration came to be held everywhere early in the morning of the day after the sabbath. As the day of the resurrection it was especially appropriate for the occurrence of the Lord's return.

Already in the time of Paul the day after the sabbath stood out from the others. This is clear from the fact that the Apostle lays down in 1 Corinthians that believers are "to lay by in store" on this day their contribution to the collection destined for the congregation at Jerusalem (1 Cor. 16 : 2).

The breaking of bread on this day is first mentioned in Acts. Paul celebrates it with the believers at Troas on his journey through that place (Acts 20 : 7). To the Didache the day after the sabbath has been appointed "the Lord's Day" in order that the Eucharist may take place on it each week (Did. 14 : 1). In the famous letter in which the younger Pliny as governor of Bithynia about 112 makes a report on the Christians to the Emperor Trajan (Pliny Ep. X : 96), he informs him that on an appointed day they gather before sunrise to sing hymns to Christ as to a god and bind themselves by an oath. Justin Martyr (100–165), in the Apology which he wrote about 150, calls the Lord's Day Sunday. He writes, on the celebration: "And on the day called the day of the sun, all who live in cities or in the country gather together in one place, and the memoirs of the apostles or the writings of the prophets are read, as long as time permits; then, when the reader has ceased, the president gives verbal instruction and an exhortation to imitate all this goodness. Then we all rise together and pray. . . . When our prayer is ended, bread and wine and water are brought, and the president in like manner offers prayers and thanksgivings, with all his might, and the people assent, saying, Amen. There is then a distribution to each" (1 Ap. 67).

The anniversary of the resurrection at Easter is even more prominent in speculation about the day of the second coming than the day of its weekly commemoration. As time went on a special importance was attached to the celebration of the eucharist at Easter. Believers all over Christendom unite on that day in looking with a special hopefulness for the return of Jesus and the appearance of the Kingdom. This presupposes that Easter is everywhere celebrated on the same day. There were difficulties about this in the Early Church. Because Easter is a moveable feast, the day on which it is to be observed can be established in different ways. The churches of Asia Minor have a different reckoning from that in use at Rome. Polycarp, the Bishop of Smyrna, travelled there shortly before his martyrdom in 156 in order to discuss the matter with Anicetus, the Bishop of Rome. About 190 the Roman Bishop Victor is demanding that the Roman dating of Easter shall be accepted by all churches. Since the Christians of Asia Minor refused, he suspended communion with them. For a century the hitherto close relations between these churches ceased altogether. At the Council of Nicaea in 325 East and West agreed that Easter should fall on the first Sunday after the spring equinox. But it was not until 525 that Rome and Alexandria came to an understanding on the reckoning of this date.

The importance of Easter, like that of baptism, has its roots in the hope of the immediate appearance of the Kingdom and the coming of Jesus in Messianic glory. Through baptism and the forgiveness of sins obtained at it, the believer acquires his claim to entry into the Kingdom. Participation in the eucharist means for him the ever-renewed experience of assurance that he belongs to the Kingdom and will share in the Messianic banquet.

The eucharist had this significance only so long as Christian belief still retained a lively expectation of the Kingdom and the return of Jesus. From the time when this was no longer true the celebration ceased to be a meal of thanksgiving and took on a meaning derived from a non-eschatological way of thinking. It then became a eucharist, a thanksgiving meal, only in name, no longer in reality. It ceased to be in any way a real meal and became a celebration in which consecrated elements are shared.

CHAPTER IV

THE KINGDOM OF GOD IN PAUL

I. PAUL'S VIEW OF THE KINGDOM OF GOD

The Kingdom is Present but Invisible

Because of the death of Jesus and their belief in his resurrection, the Apostles and primitive Christian believers expected that the Kingdom would come immediately. It was delayed. They reconciled themselves to the fact that there was an interval between the event which should have meant its appearance and its actual coming, and continued to wait.

One man, however, Paul, could not reconcile himself to the view that there must first be a period when the Kingdom is imminent. He could not do it, because he was not only a believer, but also a thinker. In him knowledge (Gnosis, γνῶσις) appears beside faith as a second authority, and demands of faith that it should acknowledge its claims. It is the great achievement of Paul that he ascribes importance to knowledge. It is from this that the special quality of the gospel he preached is derived.

What does he mean by knowledge? He means a full understanding of the meaning of the facts bearing on redemption. "We received . . . the spirit which is of God; that we might know the things that are freely given to us by God" (1 Cor. 2 : 12). "That I may know him [Christ], and the power of his resurrection, and the fellowship of his sufferings" (Phil. 3 : 10). The two main facts of redemption are Christ's death and resurrection. As the believer realizes their full consequences, he progresses from belief to knowledge. When the usual belief assumes that we can only wait for the Kingdom on the strength of the death and resurrection of Jesus, it is in error. Knowledge establishes that it must somehow have already come. In the resurrection of Jesus we are shown that the resurrection era has already appeared. It does not, however, belong to the era of this world, but to that of the Kingdom of God. That too must therefore have come already.

Knowledge is concerned, then, with the remarkable problem that the Kingdom must already be present, but that its appearance is yet to come. It is because he is dealing with this problem that Paul's doctrine of the coming of the Kingdom of God, of the Spirit, of redemption from the Law, and of the forgiveness of sins is so completely different from that of primitive Christianity, although it shares the same presuppositions. It draws the true and final consequences from them.

Paul finds the solution of the problem given in the view that, from the death and resurrection of Jesus onward, the world is in process of transformation from its temporal state into the supernatural state of the Kingdom of God. At first the Kingdom begins to achieve its realization invisibly. It remains in this state during the short period until the coming of Jesus in his glory. When this occurs it will be visible in its complete reality. The new day is therefore on the point of dawning, only the sun has not yet risen. "Now is salvation nearer to us than when we first believed" (Rom. 13 : 11). "The time is shortened" (1 Cor. 7 : 29). "The fashion of this world passeth away" (1 Cor. 7 : 31). "The Lord is at hand" (Phil. 4: 5). The transformation is being worked out in the whole of creation. In every creature there is a longing for redemption from corruption. At the appearance of the Kingdom all corruption will put on incorruption. "For the earnest expectation of the creation waiteth for the revealing of the sons of God. For the creation was subjected to vanity, not of its own will, but by reason of him who subjected it, in hope that the creation itself also shall be delivered from the bondage of corruption into the liberty of the glory of the children of God. For we know that the whole creation groaneth and travaileth in pain together until now" (Rom. 8 : 19–22).

Death and Resurrection with Christ

The transformation has progressed furthest with those who are called to the Kingdom of God. They possess a bodily nature which, like that of Jesus, undergoes in a special way the operation of the transforming powers that are at work in the age of the

Kingdom of God. What has happened with the bodily nature of Jesus is on the point of being accomplished in them. From the moment of his death and resurrection, they too have begun to undergo death and resurrection, so that they may count as having died and risen. They still wear the clothing of their natural existence. Their outer man is decaying, while the renewal of the inward man progresses day by day (2 Cor. 4 : 16). Therefore they look not at the things which are seen but at the things which are not seen (2 Cor. 4 : 18).

This mystical idea of dying and rising again with Christ, which is the basis of his view of existence in Christ and of the mystical body of Christ that embraces the believers, is developed by Paul in a number of passages; in still others he presupposes it. That baptism takes place in the name of Jesus means for him not only that the baptized belongs to him, but also that, because he belongs to Jesus Christ who died and rose again, the powers of death and resurrection are now at work in him. "Or are ye ignorant that all we who were baptized into Christ Jesus were baptized into his death? We were buried therefore with him through baptism into death: that like as Christ was raised from the dead through the glory of the Father, so we also might walk in newness of life; . . . knowing this, that our old man was crucified with him, that the body of sin might be done away" (Rom. 6 : 3–6). "Always bearing about in the body the dying of Jesus, that the life also of Jesus may be manifested in our body" (2 Cor. 4 : 10). "I have been crucified with Christ; yet I live; and yet no longer I, but Christ liveth in me" (Gal. 2 : 20). "For as many of you as were baptized into Christ did put on Christ" (Gal. 3 : 27). "One died for all, therefore all died" (2 Cor. 5 : 14). "Wherefore if any man is in Christ, he is a new creature: the old things are passed away; behold, they are become new" (2 Cor. 5 : 17).

In earlier days there was a reluctance to admit that Paul's thought was based on eschatological ideas and completely dominated by them. Interpreters therefore found themselves in the position of having constantly to undertake the hopeless task of trying to understand his strong words about dying and rising with Christ as exaggerated, picturesque description of a religious experience. It was thought that they could be explained by assuming that in his religious thought he was more influenced by the Greek mystery religions than by late Jewish eschatology. In reality the attempt to show any sign of Greek influence on him has never succeeded. The idea of rebirth which dominated late Greek religious thought is not found in him at all. He thinks of the new and higher nature of man as the result, not of a rebirth, but of an already experienced resurrection, which is thoroughly un-Greek. Nothing is thought of by Paul in figurative but everything, however paradoxical it may appear, in thoroughly concrete terms. His mysticism of existence in Christ in the form of death and resurrection with him is rooted in eschatological conceptions. It arises in an enhancement of hope for the Kingdom by which the temporal and supernatural worlds are already interwoven into one another.

In his view of the coming of the Kingdom through the death and resurrection of Jesus, Paul is in agreement with Jesus himself. It was not from him that he obtained it, for he probably never knew that he had gone to his death with the idea of bringing about the coming of the Kingdom by fulfilling the pre-Messianic tribulation in his own person, But in his exploration of the meaning of the death and resurrection of Jesus, Paul arrives at the conviction that because of them the Kingdom has already come. He holds firmly by it and seeks to develop it.

The Overthrow of the Angelic Powers

As far as its outward course is concerned, Paul sees the Kingdom of God as meaning the overcoming through Jesus Christ of the angelic beings who exercise a dominion alongside of and contrary to God's. In the late Jewish view these were responsible for the deplorable condition of the natural world. The Messiah was destined to put an end to their rule.

The defeat of the angelic beings arises from an act of ignorance which they commit. Recognizing in Jesus their adversary, they seek to get rid of him by having him crucified through the Jews. They do not know, however, that he is a being over whom they have no power. They only discover it from the fact that death does not hold him, but he rises again and so enters into his Messianic existence in which he will be their conqueror and destroyer. That the Cross became a turning-point in world history took place in accordance with the mysterious design of God for the salvation of those who love him. "We speak God's wisdom in a mystery, even the wisdom that hath been hidden, which God foreordained before the worlds unto our glory: which none of the rulers of this world knoweth: for had they known it, they would not have crucified the Lord of glory: but as it is written, Things which eye saw not, and ear heard not, and which entered not into the heart of man, whatsoever things God prepared for them that love him. But unto us God revealed them through the Spirit" (1 Cor. 2 : 7–10).

The power of the angelic beings is not the same after the death and resurrection of Jesus as it was before. This is shown in the fact that they no longer find a hearing with God as the accusers of men and can no longer hinder men's approach to God. Men's assurance that God loves them can no longer be brought into doubt. Now they have in Christ an advocate with him. "Who shall lay anything to the charge of God's elect? It is God that justifieth; who is he that shall condemn? It is Christ Jesus that died, yea rather, that was raised from the dead, who is at the right hand of God, who also maketh intercession for us. Who shall separate us from the love of Christ? Shall tribulation, or anguish, or persecution, or famine, or nakedness, or peril, or sword? . . . I am persuaded, that neither death, nor life, nor angels, nor principalities, nor things present, nor things to come, nor powers, nor height, nor depth, nor any other creature, shall be able to separate us from the love of God, which is in Christ Jesus our Lord" (Rom. 8 : 33–39).

However, the angelic powers do not yet admit defeat. With the residue of power which they still possess they prepare to resist. In particular they persecute and harass the man who is preaching the gospel of the true and wide-ranging significance of the crucifixion of Jesus and his resurrection, and consequently proclaims that their rule has thereby received its death-blow.

Paul is convinced that his plan to see the Thessalonians again was frustrated by Satan (1 Thess. 2 : 18), that the severe physical sufferings that beset him are due to an angel of Satan striking him with his fist (2 Cor. 12 : 7), and that Satan, presenting himself as an angel of light, deludes those who preach the gospel into setting up an adulterated doctrine of the death and resurrection against the true gospel which he preaches (2 Cor. 11 : 13–15).

Even the revelation of Jesus as the Messiah does not mean that the angelic powers can do no more. He has to carry on the struggle throughout the whole of time. Not until the demonic being which has the power of working death is destroyed as the last enemy is the struggle at an end.[1]

This power has already sustained a first defeat, in having to allow the resurrection of Jesus to occur. Its increasing weakness is then revealed in its inability when Jesus comes as Messiah to prevent those who belong to him through their faith from rising from the grave if they have already fallen asleep, or from being transformed into the resurrection state if they are still alive. Only at the end of the Messianic Kingdom is it destroyed, with the consequence that the general resurrection of the dead takes place and in the whole creation incorruption replaces corruption. The Kingdom of God then succeeds the Messianic.

The Messianic Kingdom and the Kingdom of God

Paul has in many respects a rather different view from Jesus of the Kingdom which thus appears at the time of the resurrection. For Jesus the Messianic Kingdom is identical with the Kingdom of God. This is shown in the fact that for him the elect not only of the final generation but of all generations belong to it. In it they are gathered together in their resurrection state.[2] Paul, on

---

[1] On the angel of death in late Jewish eschatology, see p. 38. In the Apocalypse of John death appears as a being mounted on a horse, followed by the god of hell, and granted the power to bring every form of death upon a quarter of the earth (Rev. 6 : 8).

[2] Jesus' view of the Kingdom of God goes back to that of the Apocalypse of Enoch. For this, see p. 92.

the other hand, presupposes the eschatology of the scribes, which we know from the Apocalypses of Baruch and Ezra.[3] He distinguishes, as they do, between the Messianic Kingdom and the Kingdom of God, which follows upon it. He cannot, however, adopt this distinction in the form in which it appears in the eschatology of the scribes. For them there is a profound distinction between the two kingdoms. In the Messianic there is not yet anyone risen from the dead. Only the elect of the last generation, who are still alive when it comes, have a place in it. At the general resurrection, with which the Kingdom of God appears, they enter it as those who have risen. The idea of the two kingdoms appears in Paul to this extent that he assumes that the Messianic is something by itself, that only those who belong to the final generation of men have the privilege of belonging to it, and that it lasts only for a fixed time and is then succeeded by the eternal Kingdom of God. He has, however, to correct his expectation in accordance with that of Jesus and to make the participants in the Messianic Kingdom exist in the resurrection state, either because they actually have risen from the dead, or because they have been transformed. This Kingdom then ceases to be different in kind from the Kingdom of God. It differs only in so far as those who belong to the final generation of men possess in it a blessing in advance which other generations will only enjoy later.

Paul does, however, remain entirely true to the eschatology of the scribes in assuming that in the eternal Kingdom God alone wields the power.[4] Accordingly he makes Christ at the beginning of this Kingdom give back the position and power that he holds to God, from whom he received them, and become simply a participant in the Kingdom. In this his view is not in accordance with the outlook of Jesus, so far as that is known to us. "For as in Adam all die, so also in Christ shall all be made alive. But each in his own order: Christ the first fruits; then they that are Christ's, at his coming. Then cometh the end, when he shall deliver up the Kingdom to God, even the Father; when he shall have abolished

---

[3] On this, see p. 55ff.

[4] On this doctrine of the Apocalypses of Baruch and Ezra and its importance, see p. 59f.

all rule and all authority and power. For he must reign, till he hath put all his enemies under his feet. The last enemy that shall be abolished is death. . . . And when all things have been subjected unto him, then shall the Son also himself be subjected to him that did subject all things unto him, that God may be all in all" (1 Cor. 15 : 22–28).

Where Paul finds among believers in one of his congregations the old view that in the Messianic Kingdom there are only those who were still alive when it appeared, he does not find it easy to bring them to accept the other, that believers of the final generation who have already died will enter it through the resurrection. He then bases his argument on the fact that the resurrection of Jesus is the beginning of resurrection to the Messianic Kingdom. In 1 Thessalonians he appeals to a saying of the Lord (probably referring to some revelation he has had) in support of his view of the occurrence of this first resurrection, which was later called the resurrection of the righteous. "But we would not have you ignorant, brethren, concerning them that fall asleep; that ye sorrow not, even as the rest, which have no hope. For if we believe that Jesus died and rose again, even so them also that are fallen asleep in Jesus will God bring with him. For this we say unto you by the word of the Lord, that we that are alive, that are left unto the coming of the Lord, shall in no wise precede them that are fallen asleep. For the Lord himself shall descend from heaven, with a shout, with the voice of the archangel, and with the trump of God: and the dead in Christ shall rise first: then we that are alive, that are left, shall together with them be caught up in the clouds, to meet the Lord in the air: and so shall we ever be with the Lord" (1 Thess. 4 : 13–17).

2. THE REALIZATION OF THE REIGN OF THE SPIRIT OF GOD

The Spirit as a Manifestation that the Kingdom is already Present

The transformation of the world from its natural to its supernatural state which is now in process is the realization of the Kingdom in its inward history. The idea of the transformation belongs to late Jewish eschatology and was taken over by Jesus and primitive Christianity. Jesus expects that he will be transformed into the Son of Man and that the believers will become like angels. In late Jewish eschatology, in Jesus and in primitive Christianity the transformation is thought of as taking place suddenly. Paul, on the other hand, is led to think of it as a process that takes time. He is therefore able to see the time that intervenes between the resurrection of Jesus and his return as that of the invisible development of the Kingdom which has been in existence ever since his resurrection.

Paul also adopts a different view of the Spirit from that which he found in primitive Christianity. The latter, like Judaism and the Baptist, adheres to the saying of Joel (Joel 2 : 28-32) that before the coming of the Kingdom God will pour out on all flesh his Spirit, which will enable them to prophesy and see visions. But the outpouring of the Spirit has in fact taken place only after the death and resurrection of Jesus. The primitive Christian believers attached no importance to this. They were of the opinion that they were still in the age before the coming of the Kingdom. The fact that they had received the Spirit counted to them as proof that it was near. Paul, however, is bound to attach importance to the fact that the outpouring of the Spirit has taken place after the death and resurrection of Jesus. It follows from this for him that the Spirit belongs to the age of the Kingdom of God, that it is also an indication that this is already present and that its coming has taken place because of the death and resurrection of Jesus.

It does not matter to him that he is thus putting forward a different doctrine of the Spirit from that of the tradition. It is not what has been handed down that counts as the truth about the time after the death and resurrection of Jesus, but only what is to be inferred from the fact that the death and resurrection have taken place. As he found himself compelled by this first principle of knowledge to assume that the Kingdom was somehow or other already present, so he must now proceed to see the Spirit as a manifestation of the Kingdom as already present, and try to understand what this means.

Speaking with tongues and prophesying, which were what constituted the activity of the Spirit for most believers, are for Paul only the visible signs of it. He speaks out against taking too much pride in these gifts. If the Spirit is a manifestation of the presence of the Kingdom, everything that constitutes the Kingdom must, Paul reflects, be the effect of its activity. This results in a doctrine of the Spirit which ascribes to it a far more wide-ranging activity than that which was held in primitive Christianity.

The Spirit is the power which has brought into motion and sustains the transformation of the natural into the supernatural, with which the Kingdom began and is now developing. Its activity begins in those who belong to the Kingdom. The resurrection of Jesus is the work of the Spirit dwelling in him. As the Spirit of resurrection it gives believers the capacity to rise before their time. "If the Spirit of him that raised up Jesus from the dead dwelleth in you, he that raised up Christ Jesus from the dead shall quicken also your mortal bodies through his Spirit that dwelleth in you" (Rom. 8 : 11). The Spirit is at work in them earlier than in other men. It is their destiny because they belong to Christ, all together, as the first after him, to experience the resurrection. They have "the firstfruits of the Spirit" (Rom. 8 : 23).

Jesus had already given a definitely sacramental significance to the fellowship with him enjoyed by the Galilean believers. They do not need baptism to be consecrated to entry into the Kingdom. They are already consecrated through the mere fact that, without knowing it, they have come into connexion with the future Messiah.[5]

Paul assumes that believers belong to the risen Lord in a mystical body in a way that begins at baptism. "For in one Spirit were we all baptized into one body, whether Jews or Greeks, whether bond or free" (1 Cor. 12 : 13). They have no longer any real existence of their own, but have their body in common with Christ and all other believers. Paul says that they are "the body of Christ". The expression he most commonly uses for this

[5] On Jesus' view of the significance of belonging to him, see p. 125.

is being "in Christ". Believers have a source of new vitality in the Spirit of God, which comes from Christ and flows over them. Paul therefore speaks, without making any distinction, sometimes of the Spirit of God, sometimes of the Spirit of Christ. In one instance he uses both designations together in the same passage. "But you are not in the flesh, but in the spirit, if so be that the Spirit of God dwelleth in you. But if any man hath not the Spirit of Christ, he is none of his" (Rom. 8 : 9). Being in the Spirit, believers must take pains to abide in it, in thought and conduct. If a man lives in the flesh (i.e. if he is still in his ordinary state of existence), he is giving up the existence in the Spirit through which he already belongs to the Kingdom of God, and loses everything which goes with it, including the power to rise from the dead. "If we live by the Spirit, by the Spirit let us also walk" (Gal. 5 : 25). "If ye live after the flesh, ye must die; but if by the spirit ye mortify the deeds of the body, ye shall live" (Rom. 8 : 13).

As a new vital energy the Spirit produces in believers all the special aptitudes they have. Whether they are apostles, prophets or teachers, whether they heal the sick or do some other miracle, whether they speak with tongues or are interpreters of tongues, they have everything from the Spirit (1 Cor. 12 : 27–30). Through the Spirit they are children of God. Through it they know that they are. "For as many as are led by the Spirit of God, these are sons of God. For ye received not the spirit of bondage again unto fear; but ye received the spirit of adoption, whereby we cry, Abba, Father. The Spirit himself beareth witness with our spirit, that we are children of God" (Rom. 8 : 14–16). "The love of God hath been shed abroad in our hearts through the Holy Ghost which was given unto us" (Rom. 5 : 5).

As Spirit coming from God the Spirit which is given to believers is in touch with the Spirit of God. This opens to them a way of knowledge which has existed only since the death and resurrection of Jesus. "The Spirit searcheth all things, yea, the deep things of God. For who among men knoweth the things of a man, save the spirit of the man, which is in him? Even so the things of God none knoweth, save the Spirit of God" (1 Cor. 2 : 10 f.). Through the

Spirit Paul is in touch with the risen Jesus Christ. From him he receives the answer to questions relating to the Kingdom of God. This is the source of the gospel he preaches. "For I make known to you, brethren, as touching the gospel which was preached by me, that it is not after man. For neither did I receive it from man, nor was I taught it, but it came to me through revelation of Jesus Christ" (Gal. 1 : 11 f.). His gospel consists in the knowledge of the true and full significance of the death and resurrection of Jesus. This has therefore been revealed to him by the exalted Christ. He alone is the true authority for him, not "Jesus after the flesh", as he lived in the former age when he was not yet the Messiah. That is why Paul refers only exceptionally to the tradi-tional teaching of Jesus and quotes so few of his sayings. If we had to rely on him alone we should never know that Jesus delivered the Sermon on the Mount, taught believers the Lord's Prayer and spoke parables. All that lies before the age which dawned with the death and resurrection of Jesus belongs for him to a past that has become meaningless to such an extent that he can go so far as to say, "Wherefore we henceforth know no man after the flesh: even though we have known Christ after the flesh, yet now we know him so no more" (2 Cor. 5 : 16).

Love as the Highest Gift of the Spirit

It is also from the Spirit that, according to Paul, we derive the knowledge that love constitutes the essence of the good. In sayings each surpassing the other in simplicity and warmth he repeats again and again the exhortation "Let all that you do be done in love" (1 Cor. 16 : 14). Springing from experience, they arouse the longing for a renewal of the experience. "In Christ Jesus neither circumcision availeth anything, nor uncircum-cision; but faith working through love" (Gal. 5 : 6). "The fruit of the Spirit is love, joy, peace, longsuffering, kindness, goodness, faithfulness, meekness, temperance" (Gal. 5 : 22). "Through love be servants one to another. For the whole law is fulfilled in one word, even in this; Thou shalt love thy neighbour as thyself" (Gal. 5 : 13 f.). "Bear ye one another's burdens, and so fulfil the law of Christ" (Gal. 6 : 2). "Owe no man anything, save to love one another" (Rom. 13 : 8). "And let us not be weary in well-doing" (Gal. 6 : 9). "Let us follow after things which make for peace" (Rom. 14 : 19). "Let us not be vainglorious, provoking one another, envying one another. Brethren, even if a man be overtaken in any trespass, ye which are spiritual, restore such a one in a spirit of meekness" (Gal. 5 : 26–6 : 1). "Admonish the disorderly, encourage the fainthearted, support the weak, be longsuffering toward all. See that none render unto any one evil for evil; but alway follow after that which is good, one toward another, and toward all" (1 Thess. 5 : 14 f.).

"Let love be without hypocrisy. Abhor that which is evil; cleave to that which is good. In love of the brethren be tenderly affectioned one to another; in honour preferring one another; in diligence not slothful; fervent in spirit; serving the Lord; rejoicing in hope; patient in tribulation; continuing stedfastly in prayer; communicating to the necessities of the saints; given to hospitality. Bless them that persecute you; bless, and curse not. Rejoice with them that rejoice; weep with them that weep. Be of the same mind one toward another. Set not your mind on high things, but condescend to things that are lowly. Be not wise in your own conceits. Render to no man evil for evil. Take thought for things honourable in the sight of all men. If it be possible, as much as in you lieth, be at peace with all men. Avenge not yourselves, beloved, but give place unto the wrath of God [R.V. margin]: for it is written, Vengeance belongeth unto me; I will recompense, saith the Lord. But if thine enemy hunger, feed him; if he thirst, give him to drink: for in so doing thou shalt heap coals of fire upon his head. Be not overcome of evil, but overcome evil with good" (Rom. 12 : 9–21).

The praise of love in which all these sayings are at one culminates in the hymn in 1 Corinthians. "If I speak with the tongues of men and of angels, but have not love, I am become sounding brass, or a clanging cymbal. And if I have the gift of prophecy, and know all mysteries and all knowledge; and if I have all faith, so as to remove mountains, but have not love, I am nothing. And if I bestow all my goods to feed the poor, and if I give my body to be burned, but have not love, it profiteth me nothing. Love suffereth long, and is kind; love envieth not; love vaunteth not itself, is not puffed up, doth not behave itself unseemly, seeketh not its own, is not provoked, taketh not account of evil; rejoiceth not in unrighteousness, but rejoiceth with the truth; beareth all things, believeth all things, hopeth all things, endureth all things. . . . But now abideth faith, hope, love, these three; and the greatest of these is love" (1 Cor. 13 : 1–13).

The Commandment of Love in Jesus and Paul

The ethic of love is found in the New Testament in two forms, one derived from Jesus and the other from Paul. They are quite different in their origin and their assumptions. With Jesus the ethic of love grows naturally out of the ethic of the Law which it supersedes. It is an ethic directed towards the achievement of the higher righteousness which must supplement the keeping of the Law if we are to enter the Kingdom of God. It presupposes nothing but belief in the speedy coming of the Kingdom and natural aptitude and a will to do good.

In Paul it is not an ethic directed towards entry into the Kingdom. There can be no question of this for him because in his view it cannot be obtained by the achievement of a higher righteousness but is granted by God in his grace on the basis of faith in Christ's death. For him it is proof that we are in the Kingdom. Paul presupposes the view put forward in the Apocalypses of Baruch and Ezra that men in the condition brought about by their inheritance of the sin of Adam cannot achieve the good commanded by the Law. Far less, then, can there be any question of performing acts of love required for a still higher righteousness. They can do this only when they have entered into a higher state of human existence through the granting to them of the Spirit. Their love flows from God's love poured out upon them and the whole world, "shed abroad in our hearts through the Holy Ghost" (Rom. 5 : 5). Only through this have they become capable of love.

Because the presuppositions of the ethic of love are so completely different in Paul from those of the "Christ after the flesh", he cannot preach it as if it went back to him. He has to present it entirely in his own words as something only revealed later by the Spirit which comes from Christ, and made possible only by the Spirit. This is how the ethic of love has come down to us in the form in which the historical Jesus preached it and in that which Paul received from the Spirit of Christ. If our only knowledge of Jesus had come from the Epistles of Paul, much that is irreplaceable would have been lost. But the most valuable thing of all, his ethic of love, would have been preserved for us through him. The ethic of love appears in the Christian sky in two constellations. They shine with a different light, but they both shine with the same brightness.

The ethic of love is for Paul the ethic of the Kingdom of God for the time between the resurrection of Jesus and its appearance at his return. In the state of its concealed existence it is at the same time both supernatural and ethical. The world of incorruption has not yet completely broken through that of corruption. The continued presence of corruption alongside of incorruption involves that of evil alongside of good. In the ethic of love believers have to prove that they belong to the world of the incorruptible and the good.

This compels Paul in his doctrine of the Spirit to return from the narrow doctrine of late Judaism and primitive Christianity derived from the Joel prophecy to the broader and deeper doctrine of the prophets. According to this the essence of the Kingdom lies in the fact that God has granted men an ethical spirit which enables them to act according to his will.[6] In the moving words, "The Kingdom of God is . . . righteousness and peace and joy in the Holy Ghost" (Rom. 14 : 17), Paul states clearly that for him too it is something ethical and spiritual.

In his view it is only provisionally, in the period of its concealment, that it has this character. When it appears in glory, at the return of Jesus, it will become a completely supernatural Kingdom. In this believers will pass their lives as perfect beings

[6] On the ethical conception of the Kingdom in Isaiah, Jeremiah, Ezekiel and Deutero-Isaiah, see p. 6ff.

for whom there is no longer any question of good and evil, in a state of perfect, eternal redemption from the world.

The months and years which Paul envisaged for the concealed existence of the Kingdom, in which it is an ethical and spiritual entity, have, however, become centuries. His saying about the present Kingdom which is righteousness, peace and joy in the Holy Spirit has been true for centuries and will be true for all time. Without knowing it, he has presented it to Christianity, as it was beginning to enter on its appointed pilgrimage through the ages, as its password for the journey.

The Affirmation of Work and of Earthly Institutions

Like the ethic of Jesus, that of Paul is less world-negating than we should expect in view of the way in which it is oriented to the expectation of the end of the world. Paul goes even further than Jesus in concessions to reality. In principle he agrees with his verdict that we must free ourselves from what belongs to this world in order to be prepared for that to come. But the essential thing for him is spiritual, not outward, detachment from the things of the world. It is therefore no concern of his to remould the daily life of believers so far as possible to conform with their expectation of the imminent end of the world. He does not think in terms of making the experiment of giving away one's personal possessions, or regarding work as an inopportune concern with worldly things. The saying that those who have wives should be as though they had none, those that rejoice as though they rejoiced not, those that buy as though they possessed nothing and those that use the world as not using it to the full (1 Cor. 7 : 29–31) are meant to express an inner detachment from the world. He accords an importance to work because he regards idleness as a spiritual danger. It is valuable in his eyes in so far as it confers the material independence which is essential for the moral personality. He demands it as a man who takes pride in living by his work as a weaver of canvas, instead of allowing himself to be supported by his congregations, as he had a perfect right to do. "For ye remember, brethren, our labour and travail:

working night and day, that we might not burden any of you, we preached unto you the gospel of God" (1 Thess. 2 : 9). "Study to be quiet, and to do your own business, and to work with your hands, even as we charged you; that ye may walk honestly toward them that are without, and may have need of nothing" (1 Thess. 4 : 11 f.).

What a long way Paul has come from Jesus' prohibition of anxiety about earthly things! His appreciation of work has something prophetic about it. From his innermost feelings he brings out the point of view to which Christianity was later obliged to assent, under pressure of the fact that the world was not coming to an end, but was going on. In the high value which he attaches to work Paul shows something of the mentality of modern man.

Along with the moral appreciation of activity goes a similar attitude towards order. Indiscipline is counted among the vices. He makes opposition to any kind of disorder a duty. He gives precise instructions on when and how those with gifts of the Spirit should come forward in public worship, in order that "all things be done decently and in order" (1 Cor. 14 : 40), and appeals to the fact that God is not a God of confusion, but of peace (1 Cor. 14 : 33). He constantly recommends respect for the presidents of congregations and peaceableness in all circumstances. "Admonish the disorderly" (1 Thess. 5 : 14). "But we beseech you, brethren, to know them that labour among you, and are over you in the Lord, and admonish you; and to esteem them exceeding highly in love for their work's sake" (1 Thess. 5 : 12 f.).

Because he values order as an ethical good, he finds words of recognition for its natural guardians, the magistrates. The saying of Jesus that we are to "render unto Caesar the things that are Caesar's, and unto God the things that are God's" (Mk. 12 : 13–17) is intended as irony. He slips out of the trap set by those who ask him whether taxes should be paid to Caesar with the answer that Caesar should be given what is Caesar's, and God what is God's. Its real meaning, which is not understood by its hearers, comes from the fact that, in the expectation of Jesus, very soon there will be only God and no Caesar as ruler. For Paul, however, the power of those who rule means that they are to maintain order and preserve justice by God's commission. They should be submitted to not only out of fear, but in recognition of this function of theirs. "Let every soul be in subjection to the higher powers: for there is no power but of God; and the powers that be are ordained of God. Therefore he that resisteth the power, withstandeth the ordinance of God: and they that withstand shall receive to themselves judgement. For rulers are not a terror to the good work, but to the evil . . . : for he is a minister of God to thee for good" (Rom. 13 : 1-4).

This view of the authorities comes from late Judaism. Because God's people had been living continually under foreign rule ever since the Exile, they had no real national self-consciousness, but only a religious. Foreign domination has become something they take for granted. They put up with it so long as it brings order and prosperity and does not interfere with their religion. We have written evidence of this loyal disposition right down to the time of the fixed rabbinical tradition. Through Paul it comes to be at home in Christianity.

The Atoning Death of Jesus and the Forgiveness of Sins

Like the primitive Christian believers, Paul is convinced on the basis of the application of Isaiah 53 to Jesus that his death is an atonement through which those who are called to enter the Kingdom have the assurance that they will survive the Judgement. "All have sinned . . . ; being justified freely by his [God's] grace through the redemption that is in Christ Jesus: whom God set forth to be a propitiation, through faith, by his blood" (Rom. 3 : 23-25). "For our passover also hath been sacrificed, even Christ" (1 Cor. 5 : 7).

Paul combines the view that Jesus' death establishes the forgiveness of sins with the other view, which he has in common with Jesus, and which lies at the centre of his faith, that it brings about the coming of the Kingdom. He assumes that the possibility of its coming is created by the cancellation of the existing load of guilt. Jesus has therefore ransomed believers not only

from sin, but also from the world. "Grace to you and peace from
God the Father, and our Lord Jesus Christ, who gave himself for
our sins, that he might deliver us out of this present evil world,
according to the will of our God and Father" (Gal. 1 : 3 f.).

The view of the atoning death of Jesus which he shares with
the primitive Christian believers takes on a significance for him
that goes far beyond what it meant to them. All that they gather
from it is that they will obtain the forgiveness of sins at the
Judgement. Paul, however, because of his view that the Kingdom
has already come, has to conclude that in fact they are already in it.
Because they have died and risen again with Christ, they already
belong to the Kingdom. As members of the Kingdom they
must have received also the forgiveness of sins. Because they are
living in their resurrection state, there is no question of further
sin for them. They are dead to sin and live in a new form of
existence. They are no longer under its power and subject to its
curse. "That . . we also might walk in newness of life . . . ; knowing this, that our old man was crucified with him [Christ], that
the body of sin might be done away, that so we should no longer
be in bondage to sin; for he that hath died is justified from sin"
(Rom. 6 : 4–7). "Even so reckon ye also yourselves to be dead
unto sin, but alive unto God in Christ Jesus" (Rom. 6 : 11).

Two closely linked consequences proceed from having died
and risen with Christ: emancipation from the flesh and from sin,
and the reception of the Spirit. Emancipation from death is
another consequence. Paul shares with the theology of the scribes,
which finds expression in the Apocalypse of Baruch, the view
that death came into the world through the sin of Adam.[7] Only
because the existence of the fleshy body, and so of sin, has been
suspended in believers can they partake of a premature existence
in the resurrection state at the return of Jesus, although the time
when death is stripped of all its power has not yet come. "For
the wages of sin is death" (Rom. 6 : 23). "And if Christ is in you,
the body is dead because of sin; but the spirit is life because of
righteousness" (Rom. 8 : 10). "If ye live after the flesh, ye must
die" (Rom. 8 : 13).

[7] On this, see p. 56f.

Freedom from the Law

Along with emancipation from the flesh, from sin and from death, freedom from the Law is also obtained in dying and rising with Christ. For Paul it is part of the correct understanding of the forgiveness of sins, attained through knowledge, that the Law has been invalidated through the death of Jesus. In this he finds himself in opposition to primitive Christianity, which did not draw this conclusion from the death of Jesus.

In Paul's view the death of Jesus meant an end to the Law. For him this follows from the nature of this death. According to the Law, everyone who hangs on a tree is accursed (Deut. 21 : 23). Jesus, when he was crucified, hung upon a tree. Therefore he would have to be accursed. Since this cannot be true, the Law is shown to be no longer valid (Gal. 3 : 13 f.). The fact that here comes to light has its real ground in the limitation by which the Law is valid only till the age of the Kingdom of God. This is also the view of the scribes. The idea that the Law might have ceased to be valid had not occurred to the primitive Christian believers, who thought that they were still living in the age of expectancy of the coming of the Kingdom. Paul, however, because of his knowledge that the Kingdom was already present in consequence of the death and resurrection of Jesus, had then to assert that the Law was no longer valid and to oppose the view that Gentile Christians were under any obligation to take it upon themselves. Unfortunately he could not do this by simply representing it as something that had become unimportant and unnecessary, with which Gentile believers need not be burdened. He had to make the tremendous claim that to take over the Law would cost them their salvation. This drew upon him the opposition of the original apostles, the Jewish Christians and the Jews, and resulted in his martyrdom.

This remarkable conception of the Law is based upon the fact that in Paul's opinion the Law was not given to the people by God, but by the angels (Gal. 3 : 19 f.). In this he is not alone. Stephen makes the same assumption in his speech before the high council (Acts 7 : 53), and so does the writer of the Epistle to the Hebrews (Heb. 2 : 2). This view is also attested by Josephus (Ant. XV : 52). The explanation of its appearance is that in late Judaism God had come to be thought of as such a completely transcendent being that it was hard to conceive of his having direct dealings with men. Thus the view came to be developed, particularly among the scribes at Alexandria, that wherever the scripture reported God's dealings with men, it was to be understood in the sense that it took place through the medium of angels.

From the theory that the Law had been given by angels, Paul draws very different conclusions from the other representatives of this view. He goes on to claim that the obedience demanded to the Law does not concern God but only the angels. From this he draws the conclusion that the existence of the Law points to the presence of angelic dominion. Accordingly to subject those who had previously been Gentiles to the Law after they had become Christians means, in Paul's view, nothing less than handing them over to the dominion of the angelic powers just at the moment when these are about to become impotent, handing them over to the rule of the enemies with whom Christ is locked in struggle, because they are holding up the coming of the Kingdom and trying to stop men from taking the road to it. In taking over the Law, Gentile believers are therefore, without knowing it, giving up their existence in Christ and so losing their calling to belong to the Kingdom. It is because in his opinion this is a matter of an error fraught with such momentous consequences that Paul attacks it with such passion.

The view that the Law could not enable man to attain the righteousness it holds before him was also held in some rabbinical circles of the day. It is found in the Apocalypses of Baruch and Ezra and is there based on the view that the sinfulness man has inherited from Adam is responsible for it. Because of this the Law cannot help him to become good, but can only hold the vision of the good before him and so bring him to an awareness of his sinfulness.[8]

Paul was probably acquainted with this view of the Law before his conversion, just as he also presupposes the eschatology rep-

[8] On this, see p. 57.

resented in the Apocalypses of Baruch and Ezra. He is far from concluding from the fact that the Law was given by angels that it is bad in itself. It is good. Only it can be of no help to man in his sinfulness. It was not because they desired their well-being but because they desired their misery that the angels gave the Law to God's people. They keep them at the attractive-looking but hopeless task of trying to fulfil the Law in order to keep them under their sway. They leave the people believing that by striving to keep the Law they are proving themselves to be God's people, when in reality it is ensuring that the people belong to them. Now with the death and resurrection of Jesus the Kingdom, and so the end of the Law, has come. Accordingly wherever Paul preaches this and shows the true way to enter the Kingdom of God, the angelic powers try successfully to bring into the field against his gospel of truth the gospel of ignorance. Again and again the true gospel finds itself involved in controversy with those who cannot rid themselves of an error whose appeal comes from its very simplicity. It is the view that, in order to participate in the Kingdom, something more than faith in Jesus is required. It is necessary, in this view, also to acquire membership in the Jewish people by fulfilling all the requirements, and to strive for the righteousness which is according to the Law. In his zeal for freedom from the Law Paul makes use of all the arguments at his disposal and also of the concept of justification by faith as the counterpart of justification by works of the Law, a concept which he has forged as the most suitable weapon for this combat. "But now apart from the law a righteousness of God hath been manifested, being witnessed by the law and the prophets; even the righteousness of God through faith in Jesus Christ" (Rom. 3 : 21 f.). "We reckon therefore that a man is justified by faith apart from the works of the law" (Rom. 3 : 28).

It was long assumed that this doctrine of justification granted by God purely on the basis of faith in the atoning death of Jesus must have been the centrepiece of Paul's doctrine of the forgiveness of sins. It is not. The doctrine of forgiveness which really occupies his heart and mind is that which comes from the mystical view of dying and rising again with Jesus. This embraces and explains everything that constitutes participation in the Kingdom which is beginning to come into existence: possession of the Spirit and emancipation from existence in the flesh, from sin, from death and from the Law. For it is also necessary to have died and risen again with Christ to obtain emancipation from the Law. We die to the Law, as we do to the flesh, to sin and to death. "For I through the law died unto the law, that I might live unto God" (Gal. 2 : 19).

The idea of justification through faith alone without works of the Law goes back to that of the atoning death of Jesus, which is its sole foundation. The conviction of freedom from the Law which it brings with it is not in itself included in the idea of the atoning death of Jesus. Paul cannot have derived it from this. He inserts it into it. How did he become convinced of the connexion between freedom from the Law and the forgiveness of sins? From the mystical doctrine of existence in Christ, at which he arrived through his special knowledge. The idea of the forgiveness of sins and that of freedom from the Law are both alike based on this in the wonderful passage in Romans: "There is therefore now no condemnation to them that are in Christ Jesus. For the law of the Spirit of life in Christ Jesus made me free from the law of sin and of death" (Rom. 8 : 1 f.).

Paul's real doctrine of the forgiveness of sins is therefore that which arises out of the mysticism of having died and risen with Christ. The doctrine of justification by faith alone, without works of the Law, is only a short, incomplete formulation of this, used by him where he is dealing with the question of the Law.

Of course Paul too takes for granted a continuous effort to do what is good. The only thing is that it must not give rise to the idea that redemption can be obtained in this way. Once this has been granted in the form of existence in Christ won through faith and baptism, the doing of good necessarily follows in consequence of possession of the Spirit and as a proof of it. In Paul there can be no faith without works. They are the fruit it bears. If they are lacking, or begin to be lacking, it means that the faith from which life in Christ and the possession of the Spirit come is not present, or has ceased to be present. Redemption cannot be won through works. But to remain redeemed and not produce works is inconceivable. If therefore the writer of the Epistle of James is really engaging in polemic against Paul in his saying that faith without works is dead (Jam. 2 : 17), he is doing him an injustice. Paul thinks just the same.

This doctrine of Paul's about the Law is complicated, though from the point of view of the eschatological outlook it is thoroughly logical. It is complicated still further by the fact that, while Gentile believers must not adopt the Law, Jewish believers ought to go on observing it.

This remarkable attitude which Paul demands towards a Law which is no longer valid is the application of a principle which he has further established and which he follows in other questions too. It lays down that the believer should remain in the outward condition in which he was first converted. "As the Lord hath distributed to each man, as God hath called each, so let him walk. And so ordain I in all the churches" (1 Cor. 7 : 17). "Let each man abide in that calling wherein he was called" (1 Cor. 7 : 20). If a man was a slave when he became a believer, he should not, on this theory, accept freedom even if it is offered him (1 Cor. 7 : 21 f.). If he was married when he became a believer, he should remain married and not allow himself to be talked into the view that he and his wife must now live as if they were not married in order to achieve sanctification for the coming Kingdom (1 Cor. 7 : 3-5, 10 f.). If anyone was single or widowed, that is how he should stay, and he should do so because he is better off in this condition, in so far as he can direct his thoughts entirely towards Christ, whereas those who are married are subject to the claims of their human dependants (1 Cor. 7 : 8, 32-35). In the same way he who was called as a non-Jew should remain a non-Jew and he who was called as a Jew must not take any steps to count as a non-Jew (1 Cor. 7 : 18).

This theory of the *status quo* is required by the mysticism of existence in Christ. From the moment anyone is in Christ, his true nature is entirely determined by this. His natural form of existence and everything that goes with it have become meaningless. He is like a house sold for demolition: there is no longer any question of alterations.

The fact that, in consequence of this theory, some are told to do what is forbidden to others exposes it to misunderstandings on both sides. One party claims that Paul is leading the Jews who live among the Gentiles to abandon the Law (Acts 21 : 21); on the other hand, as we know from Galatians, there were some who circulated the rumour that he was still preaching the Law which he was withholding from the Gentile Christians (Gal. 5 : 11). At any rate this attitude on the question of the Law imposed upon him by the theory of the *status quo* made it easy for his opponents to confuse his congregations.

The Complete and the Continuing Forgiveness of Sins

According to Paul's doctrine, therefore, the believer is already in possession of a complete forgiveness of sins. It comes not only from the fact that he enjoys the forgiveness leading to entry into the Kingdom, which has been won by Jesus through his atoning death, but also from the fact that in dying and rising again with Christ the believer is dead to sin. This forgiveness of sins is not, however, complete in the sense that he can expect because of it to have forgiveness for all the sins that he commits in his whole life. Paul fully adheres to the primitive Christian view that the forgiveness of sins won by Jesus' atoning death and granted to believers at baptism only applies to sins committed before baptism. It is a total, but not a continuing forgiveness.

The primitive Christian and the Pauline view of baptism have an objective character into which we have to think ourselves. It is an event having reference to the coming of the Kingdom. The individual shares in it through faith in Jesus and the baptism in which he is accepted into the fellowship of those who are to enter the Kingdom. There is no thought of an effort to obtain the assurance of forgiveness and a struggle to receive it intellectually, such as Luther presupposes. Paul shares the primitive Christian view that believers are saints in virtue of their baptism.[9]

[9] On the replacement of the term "righteous" by "saints" in Daniel, see p. 30.

He addresses them as such in his Epistles. His theory that the Kingdom has already come, and that they are living in it as already dead and risen with Christ, is the basis of the condition of sanctity in which they find themselves. At the time when Christian baptism arose, it could be assumed that they would remain in this condition simply because, in view of the proximity of the Kingdom, there would be no time for further acts of sin. Paul, writing two decades later, makes it possible to understand that, with the right will, they still had the capability of remaining in it.

He cannot, however, avoid the conviction that believers do relapse from life according to the Spirit to life after the flesh. The antedating of the arrival of the Kingdom and of the resurrection state as that appropriate for believers comes into conflict with reality.

These are the facts which give rise to the problem of whether sins committed after baptism can be forgiven. Paul never comes to grips with it in its full range and all its difficulty. He seeks to check this relapse into sin by urging believers to realize its consequences. He reminds them by way of warning how many Israelites who had expected to reach the promised land were deprived of it and perished because of their sin during the journey through the wilderness (1 Cor. 10 : 1–13). Twice (1 Cor. 6 : 9–11 and Gal. 5 : 19–21) he specifies the sins of which it is certain "that they which practise such things shall not inherit the Kingdom of God". They are, above all, fornication, idolatry, adultery, theft, covetousness, slander, wrath, strife, jealousy, drunkenness and revelling. He never mentions by name any believers who have forfeited the Kingdom by sinning in this way.

He does not even convict the member of the congregation at Corinth who had committed a grave sin of unchastity by name. He contents himself with the instruction that the whole congregation assembled in the name of Jesus shall deliver this sinner to Satan "for the destruction of the flesh, that the spirit may be saved in the day of the Lord Jesus" (1 Cor. 5 : 1–5). He does not therefore give up this sinner, who strictly should have forfeited the Kingdom, as lost, but assumes that he will expiate his sin in the torments which he undergoes from Satan. He knows that to be delivered to Satan means physical suffering. The severe handicap that is his own lot he explains as ill-treatment at the hands of an angel of Satan, so that he "should not be exalted overmuch by reason of the exceeding greatness of the revelations" accorded to him (2 Cor. 12 : 7).

Only one sin counts for him as completely unforgivable: that of falsifying the gospel by the doctrine that Gentile believers should be made to take the Law upon themselves. He refers to those who are guilty of this as men who have no longer any hope of entering the Kingdom. "He that troubleth you shall bear his judgement, whosoever he be" (Gal. 5 : 10). "Ye are severed from Christ, ye who would be justified by the law; ye are fallen away from grace" (Gal. 5 : 4). "For many walk, of whom I told you often, and now tell you even weeping, that they are the enemies of the cross of Christ: whose end is perdition" (Phil. 3 : 18). This sin is for him the greatest of all, because its effects are not limited to him who commits it, but will give occasion to others too to relapse into walking after the flesh and neglect the redemption that has come through Christ.

The reason why Paul does not really go into the problem of whether sins committed after baptism can be forgiven is that he expects the Kingdom, and with it the end of sin, quite soon and leaves the decision to Christ, who is coming to hold the Judgement.

CONCLUDING THOUGHTS

THE EXPECTATION AND THE REALIZATION
OF THE KINGDOM OF GOD

The idea of the Kingdom as already present and developing appeared alongside that of the Kingdom of pure expectation in the very earliest age of Christianity and strove to replace it. Paul comes to the conclusion that it must somehow have come already, when he comes to deal with the fact of its non-appearance. In the effort to grasp the fact that it must have come in Jesus' death and resurrection and nevertheless has not yet openly appeared, he finds the explanation in the assumption that it is at first invisible. In a transformation of the temporal into the supernatural world which is already in progress, it is developing into the Kingdom which will shortly make its visible appearance. The primitive Christian believers were quite unable to understand this view, well-founded in its own way, although it arose and is quite intelligible in the burning expectation of the Kingdom which they shared with Paul.[1]

They opposed it fiercely because it had consequences which were unacceptable to them. In the generations that followed there was no possibility whatever of its finding acceptance. The burning primitive Christian expectation of the Kingdom, without which it cannot be understood, no longer existed. It seemed destined from every point of view to have no future. In itself, indeed, it had none. But it has remained preserved in the Epistles of Paul. From them, without being acknowledged or understood, and as a doctrine of the already present Kingdom of God, it has exercised in succeeding centuries a unique influence on the formation of the Christian faith through the ideas and presuppositions that are bound up with it.

The importance which the doctrine of the Spirit that Paul created has had, still has and always will have is immeasurable. What would have become of Christianity if it had had to take its

[1] On the considerations on which this view is based, see p. 154ff.

course through the centuries with the inadequate primitive Christian conception of the Spirit, who indicated the nearness of the Kingdom by the prophesying and speaking with tongues which are his special activity? With nothing to point to but these, the problems which arose as the expectation of the Kingdom moved from the near to the remote future could never have been solved. As it was, Paul's conception of the Spirit as the new vital energy coming from faith in Christ gave it the possibility of claiming and understanding that redemption was already present. Whenever in the course of the centuries the doctrine of the Spirit is under consideration, it is Paul who dominates the discussion.

Another unique gift which Christianity has received from Paul is his doctrine of the forgiveness of sins. His conviction that it can be obtained direct from God by faith in the atoning death of Jesus lives on in later times, side by side with the other doctrine that the mediation of the Church and acts which she requires the sinner to perform are requisite. In Protestantism it established itself as a doctrine of continuous forgiveness of sins. The rise of this faith in continuous forgiveness depends upon the doctrine of justification by faith. Without it it could never have arisen. The wonderful words in which Paul pronounces the blessedness of possessing complete forgiveness kept alive in succeeding generations a longing for such an experience. This mood led to the development out of the concept of the reception of the forgiveness of sins through faith alone the idea of a forgiveness which could be obtained continually. With this the gravest problem with which Christianity had had to deal since the beginning found a solution in the sixteenth century. Who can estimate the comfort that the words, "There is therefore now no condemnation to them that are in Christ Jesus" (Rom. 8 : 1) have given through the centuries to broken hearts?

A deep and inward piety, existing alongside the ecclesiastical, has its roots in the gospel of Paul and has been handed down from generation to generation. Those who know it find edification in those strange-looking words about being in Christ, dying and rising with him, walking in a new state of existence. They do not know what they originally meant. Nor can they give them any very clear meaning. They seem to them like incomprehensible parables of spiritual experience. They are felt as something special, not to be compared with anything else, and not found anywhere but in Paul. Through them men find strength, light, peace, joy, quietness and comfort. They walk with them on the peaks of faith. They receive all this from them because they are words in which he who was the first to reach the knowledge that it must have already come is speaking of the blessedness of life in the Kingdom.

Because Paul is a thinker as well as a believer, he wishes to pass from expectation of the Kingdom to experience of it. He deems it incompatible with the view that Jesus is the bringer of the Kingdom (and Jesus saw himself as such) that it should not come at once. Dominated by this conviction, he experienced in the spirit its present reality in the imagery of his time. The expectation of the Kingdom which would come of itself was not to find actual fulfilment. For centuries Christianity looked for it in vain. It could not easily come to terms with the fact. It had to try to understand what could be learned from it. When it applied itself to the interpretation of the signs of the times, it could understand them only as meaning that it was called upon to renounce its old ideas and learn anew. The task was laid upon it of giving up its belief in the Kingdom which would come of itself and giving its devotion to the Kingdom which must be made real.

Paul the thinker recognized as the essence of the Kingdom of God which was coming into existence that it consists in the rule of the Spirit. We learn from this knowledge which comes to us through him that the way in which the coming of the Kingdom will be brought about is by the coming of Jesus Christ to rule in our hearts and through us in the whole world. In the thought of Paul the supernatural Kingdom is beginning to become the ethical and with this to change from the Kingdom to be expected into something which has to be realized. It is for us to take the road which this prospect opens up.

INDEX OF PASSAGES

INDEX OF PROPER NAMES